The Black Arcl

THE TIME
WARRIOR

By Matthew Kilburn

Published October 2018 by Obverse Books

Cover Design © Cody Schell

Text © Matthew Kilburn, 2018

Range Editors: Paul Simpson, Philip Purser-Hallard, Stuart Douglas

For my parents, Doreen and Alan, and sister Jessica

Also Available

CONTENTS

OVERVIEW

Serial Title: *The Time Warrior*

Writer: Robert Holmes

Director: Alan Bromly

Original UK Transmission Dates: 15 December 1973 – 5 January 1974

Running Time:	
	Part One: 24m 15s
	Part Two: 24m 10s
	Part Three: 23m 30s
	Part Four: 24m 57s

UK Viewing Figures:	Part One: 8.7 million
	Part Two: 7.0 million
	Part Three: 6.6 million
	Part Four: 10.6 million

Regular Cast: Jon Pertwee (The Doctor), Elisabeth Sladen (Sarah Jane Smith), Nicholas Courtney (Brigadier Lethbridge-Stewart)

Guest Cast: Kevin Lindsay (Linx), David Daker (Irongron), John J Carney (Bloodaxe), Alan Rowe (Edward of Wessex), June Brown (Eleanor), Gordon Pitt (Eric), Jeremy Bulloch (Hal), Sheila Fay (Meg), Donald Pelmear (Professor Rubeish), Steve Brunswick (Sentry)

Antagonists: Linx, Irongron

Novelisation: *Doctor Who and the Time Warrior* by Terrance Dicks. **The Target Doctor Who Library** #65.

Responses:

'*The Time Warrior* destroys the lie that the Pertwee era got worse as it went along, and remains one of the series' most entertaining serials.'

[Joe Ford, *Doc Oho*]

'This story is poor and thin. It's written tongue-in-cheek, but directed without any awareness of... well, anything. The result is simply dull.'

[Finn Clark, *The Doctor Who Ratings Guide*]

Synopsis

Part One

In the Middle Ages, a group of criminals led by the bandit **Irongron** discover a crashed spaceship belonging to Sontaran warrior **Linx**, who claims Earth for his empire and offers Irongron 'magic' weapons in return for shelter. Irongron and his second-in-command **Bloodaxe** agree to the deal despite not trusting Linx.

Brigadier Lethbridge-Stewart has brought **the Doctor** in to investigate the disappearance of scientists from a top secret research complex. He meets journalist **Sarah Jane Smith**, who is posing as her aunt, virologist Lavinia Smith, in search of a story, as well as **Professor Rubeish**, an extremely shortsighted scientist. Linx has been kidnapping the scientists, and takes Rubeish back in time. The Doctor follows in the TARDIS, unaware Sarah has stowed away.

Lady Eleanor, the wife of Irongron's neighbour, **Edward of Wessex**, sends her archer **Hal** to assassinate the bandit, but his aim is thrown by the arrival of Sarah who is captured by Irongron's men. The Doctor sees this, and then witnesses Linx removing his helmet to reveal his true form.

Part Two

Sarah believes she is at some sort of reenactment and refuses to take Irongron seriously, but Linx hypnotises her and is concerned to discover that someone has followed him back through time. Sarah sneaks away, and Linx gives Irongron a robot fighter which the bandit decides to use against Hal. However the Doctor manages to break the robot's control box, allowing Hal, with Sarah's help, to escape. Hal takes Sarah back to Wessex Castle, where she tells Lady Eleanor that she is sure the Doctor is a magician helping Irongron. She and Hal return to Irongron's castle to kidnap the Doctor.

The Doctor manages to get inside Linx's underground lair, where the missing scientists have been hypnotised and are working on repairing his spacecraft. Rubeish's poor eyesight means he is unaffected, but he is fascinated by Linx's work. The Sontaran captures the Doctor and, ignoring the Time Lord's concerns about interfering with history, puts him to work. Rubeish frees the Doctor but he runs into Bloodaxe and Irongron, who threatens him with an axe.

Part Three

Hal and Sarah rescue the Doctor, and take him back to Wessex Castle, where he agrees to help defend the place against an imminent attack by Irongron. He suggests using dummies to make it seem there are more defenders, and brews up some stink bombs with Sarah's aid.

Linx accompanies the bandits and encourages them to use the new rifles he has provided; when these reveal the dummies, the Doctor deploys the smoke bombs which causes Irongron and his men to retreat. The Doctor counsels Sir Edward to capture Irongron's castle, and asks Lady Eleanor's help in obtaining herbs to make a sleeping draught.

The next day, the Doctor and Sarah pose as friars to enter the enemy lair, and then make their way down to Linx's laboratory. The Doctor works out how to dehypnotise the scientists, and while Sarah and

Rubeish begin to do so, he offers to assist Linx with the repairs – if all the evidence of Linx's presence is destroyed when the Sontaran leaves. In reply, Linx fires his gun at the Doctor.

Part Four

Sarah saves the Doctor by attacking Linx. Rubeish hits the Sontaran in his one vulnerable spot, on the probic vent. To buy time for the dehypnotising, the Doctor poses as the robot knight, demonstrating its abilities to Irongron. However, his ruse is discovered, and the bandit decides to use the Doctor for target practice for his men.

Sarah tries to steal some food from Irongron's kitchen for the starving scientists, but is caught – however, this gives her the opportunity to put the sleeping draught in the stew. Irongron retrieves Linx from where the Doctor and Sarah had left him tied up, and just as Linx loses patience with the bandits' incompetent firing, Sarah helps the Doctor escape. They return to Wessex Castle to wait for the sleeping potion to take effect.

By the time it starts to overpower the bandits, Linx is ready to depart, and the Doctor and Sarah arrive just in time to start sending the scientists back to the 20th century with Linx's osmic projector. Irongron believes Linx is responsible for a spell bewitching his men but the Sontaran kills him. As Linx enters his spaceship, Hal looses an arrow that hits the Sontaran's probic vent, killing him – but not before he prematurely activates the controls.

Roused by Hal, Bloodaxe and the others flee the castle, which is destroyed by Linx's spaceship exploding. The Doctor and Sarah head back to the TARDIS.

INTRODUCTION: DISCOVERING AND REDISCOVERING HISTORY IN DOCTOR WHO

'A straight line may be the shortest distance between two points, but it is by no means the most interesting.'

(The Doctor, *The Time Warrior*, Part One)

From the standpoint of **Doctor Who**'s self-presentation in the early 1970s, and certainly from the point of view of those familiar with the directions **Doctor Who** has taken since its return to television in 2005, the realisation that *The Time Warrior* (1973-74) is the first story of the 1970s to take place in Earth's historical past is a surprising and even disorienting one. Indeed, the previous serial to have any section set in the British past was *The Evil of the Daleks* (1967) six years earlier, with *The Abominable Snowmen* (1967) two stories after it inhabiting a 1930s Tibet which made the most minimal of acknowledgements to its historical and geographical setting. Between then and the commissioning of *The Time Warrior* in 1973, **Doctor Who** had undergone several transformations both within its narrative and in the context of its surrounding cultural landscape. However, time travel had not been forgotten in the interim, nor had the programme's attachment to ideas of history and the Doctor's place as an explorer in the human past.

The period was almost bookended by two stories which employed the 'past' but which transplanted that past to otherworldly and futuristic settings. The first of these was *The War Games* (1969), whose First World War, Western Front, location turned out to be one of many 'time zones' on another world to which combatants from wars in Earth's history had been transplanted. There, aliens could manage the trajectories of sections of the conflicts and then assemble a supposedly unassailable army from survivors. The second was *Carnival of Monsters* (1973), where the arrival of the Doctor and Jo on the *SS Bernice* in 1926 – a famous missing vessel, the Doctor reports at the beginning of the story – turns out to be on a miniaturised ship held with many other specimens of times, places and species within a Miniscope, a futuristic peepshow being exhibited by down-at-heel carnival entertainers. Both stories blurred genres while pointing out the artificiality of the period historical drama itself, in this case presenting people who are diegetically 'real' within the fiction as unwitting actors in a play staged by external forces[1].

The War Games was co-written by Terrance Dicks, who as script editor of **Doctor Who** from 1968 to 1974 oversaw both *Carnival of Monsters* and *The Time Warrior*. *Carnival of Monsters* was written by Robert Holmes, whose first **Doctor Who** serial, *The Krotons* (1968) was Dicks' first 'solo project' as editor. *The Time Warrior* was Holmes' next broadcast **Doctor Who** story after *Carnival of Monsters*. Both *The War Games* and *Carnival of Monsters* set precedents for the way *The Time Warrior* treated 'real' history by acknowledging the artificiality of television drama. Whether by accident or design, this placed a particular reading upon the **Doctor Who** historical as it operated between 1964 and 1967. These historical stories

---

[1] For a useful discussion of genre in **Doctor Who** historicals and self-conscious artifice see O'Mahony, Daniel, '"Now How is That Wolf Able to Impersonate a Grandmother?" History, Pseudo-history and Genre in **Doctor Who**' in Butler, David, ed, *Time And Relative Dissertations In Space*, p56-67.

emphasise the Doctor and his fellow TARDIS travellers as intermediaries for the viewer, spectators of and participants in historical action without being truly of the society which they were visiting. *The War Games* and *Carnival of Monsters* enhance this inheritance by including viewers within their narratives, in the forms of the army-assembling aliens in one and the fairground hucksters Vorg and Shirna and their official interrogators on Inter Minor in the other. Both groups discover the Doctor and his friend or friends are intruders in their 'programme', spurring a battle for narrative control. *The Time Warrior* works in a comparable way. The Doctor's antagonist, Linx, has the defined aim of seeking to repair his spaceship and return to his war with the Rutans, and treats the planet and historical period in which he finds himself as a form of entertainment, writing a new script for his hosts and giving them new props. The conflict between Irongron on one side and Sir Edward and Lady Eleanor on the other dramatically mirrors the off-screen Sontaran-Rutan War, from which they are a sidestep from Linx's viewpoint.

Robert Holmes and Terrance Dicks tended to discuss *The Time Warrior* as an innovation, as did the third principal creative force on the serial, producer Barry Letts. While it undoubtedly began the mid-1970s rediscovery of the past as a setting by **Doctor Who**, the form of 'a history story with a strong science-fiction element'[2] had been pioneered during the programme's second year with *The Time Meddler* (1965) and followed with the ancient Egypt section ('Golden Death' and 'Escape Switch', episodes 9 and 10 (both 1966)) of *The Daleks' Master Plan* (1965-66) and *The Evil of the Daleks* (1967). The emergence of fan-led study of **Doctor Who** in the late 1970s

---

[2] Barry Letts, interviewed in 'Beginning the End' (DVD extra).

identified *The Time Meddler* as the founder of the 'pseudo-historical' genre[3], an idea transmitted to a wider audience in the early 1980s through the commercially published *Doctor Who Monthly* (DWM)[4].

Between *The War Games* and *The Time Warrior*, history was principally represented in **Doctor Who** as a realm from which the Doctor was cut off. Recollections of his encounters with historical figures became part of the characterisation of the third Doctor, enhanced in delivery by Jon Pertwee's ability as a raconteur. They also emphasised the Doctor as wistful and frustrated, longing for the resumption of his adventuring in time and space. In the absence of dramatised time travels for the viewer to enjoy, the Doctor's conversation emphasised not just his otherworldliness but his extratemporality, while anchoring him to human affairs. His remarks suggested an aversion to political murder as an instrument of change, as in his launching into an anecdote about (presumably) Edward VII (*Inferno*, 1970)[5], while a willingness to celebrate past comradeship with revolutionary figures such as Mao (*The Mind of Evil* (1971)) and Napoleon (*Day of the Daleks*, (1972)) as well as a British military hero such as Nelson (*The Sea Devils*, (1972)), suggests a traveller's cosmopolitanism at odds with the institutional settings in which he was placed, but also an attitude sympathetic to the ideals of post-war social democracy in Britain without necessarily tolerating how this worked in practice.

There was also a strand of stories in which a science-fictional

---

[3] Wiggins, Martin J, 'Artificial History', *TARDIS* vol 6 nos 3&4, October 1981.

[4] 'The Visitation', *Doctor Who Monthly* (DWM) #62, March 1982.

[5] 'Pity. A charming family. I knew her great-grandfather in Paris. Do you know, I remember on one occasion –' (*Inferno*, Episode 3).

element in the historic and prehistoric past interrupted everyday life on 20th-century Earth as much as an outer-space invasion. *Doctor Who and the Silurians* (1970), *The Dæmons* (1971) and *The Sea Devils* all fit into this category. *The Time Monster* (1972) is an outlier because its portrayal of Atlantis rejects **Doctor Who**'s conventional sense of the historical and embraces the speculative and mythological. The presence of a beast such as the Minotaur places its Atlantis firmly in the fantastical, but at the same time the programme seeks a historical Atlantis on the island of Thera (Santorini), where the destruction of the Bronze Age settlement at Akrotiri by a volcanic eruption in the late 17th century BCE was fashionable in the early 1970s as a historical precedent for Plato's story of the destruction of Atlantis. *The Time Warrior* would play less self-consciously with the historical, the fictional, and medieval history as folklore. *The Time Warrior* is a successor to *The Dæmons* and *The Time Monster* in that the nature of the threat can be summarised as an alien experimenting with human history, but this would obscure the individual motivation of Linx, which characterises this story's break with the cosmic-scale morality favoured by earlier third Doctor past/present tales in favour of one which depends on more tightly focused ethical choices.

The return of the pseudohistorical story was also a consequence of changes in **Doctor Who**'s fictional narrative which reversed trends set in motion in 1966, but which could not return to the 1963-66 status quo as their end point. In the first year of **Doctor Who**'s production, stories were divided between 'Past', 'Future', and 'Sideways'[6]. In the end, *The Edge of Destruction* (1964), and *Planet of Giants* (1964), were the only two broadcast serials designated as

---

[6] O'Mahony, '"Now How is that Wolf…"', p58.

'Sideways'[7]. As the Doctor's quest for most of the first four years of the series was to return one or more of his companions to their own time – first Ian and Barbara, then (with less urgency) Dodo, and then Polly and Ben, the present day had to be an elusive destination, to be reached only by proxies for the TARDIS – first the Time and Space Visualiser and then the Dalek time machine in *The Chase* (1965) – or fleetingly, as in the visit to a cricket match in *The Daleks' Master Plan* on New Year's Day 1966.

The War Machines (1966) saw the programme renege on a pact with itself and allowed the Doctor to return to, or at least near, the year of broadcast. Subsequent visits to the present day or near-present in the remainder of the 1960s – always England and mainly London or nearby – such as *The Faceless Ones* (1967), part of *The Evil of the Daleks*, *The Web of Fear* (1968), *Fury from the Deep* (1968) and *The Invasion* (1968), were supplemented by serials set at various removes into Earth's future such as *The Ice Warriors* (1967), *The Enemy of the World* (1967-68) and *The Seeds of Death* (1969). The pairing of the second Doctor for most of his run with companions who were not from 1960s Britain but from the past or from a future at a significant remove from our own made him into the audience's representative of modernity to an extent never enjoyed by his predecessor. He explains the electric power source of the London Underground to Jamie and Victoria in *The Web of Fear* and 'Euro Sea Gas' to them in *Fury from the Deep*. In *The Invasion*, Jamie and Zoe struggle a little to find their feet in a world of photography and transistor radios, but again the Doctor is au fait with everything. The past was sublimated into aspects of design, such as the Viking

---

[7] Whitaker, David, 'Doctor Who. Serial Details... Story Details', 1964, BBC WAC, T5/647/1.

influence on the Ice Warriors or the 'Homeric' costumes of the space police force in *The Space Pirates* (1969)[8].

The eclipse of stories set in the past in favour of stories set in the present and near future also saw a decline in the number of stories set on other worlds. This refocusing on a present and future Earth made the second Doctor's period as appropriate for the tagline, 'Adventures in the Human Race', if not more so, than the 2005 series of **Doctor Who** for which it was designed. However, in season five these were forward-looking adventures in worlds of technology, and even when more variety crept in season six, history was a source for fantasy, as in the literary creations with whom the Doctor and his companions conversed in *The Mind Robber* (1968). The second Doctor was an avuncular figure of authority who interpreted depictions of the audience's present day and their future to Jamie, Victoria and Zoe. The third Doctor initially presented a more dependent figure. Without a functioning TARDIS and thus the ability to leave the scene of an adventure without accountability (a rapid departure from each adventure without saying goodbye to the people he has helped becoming part of the Doctor's methodology from *The War Machines* onwards), the Doctor's status in each serial in season seven has to be earned by overcoming his selfishness and his boredom, applying his knowledge, and delivering results. Brigadier Lethbridge-Stewart, as his employer, is a more powerful force, replacing the Doctor as the apex of a character triangle.

The third Doctor was progressively strengthened, firstly by the reshuffling and enlargement of the ensemble cast for season eight.

---

[8] Wiggins, Martin, 'Out of Time', *Circus* 9, Spring 2002, citing Hood, Stuart, 'Who does it?' *The Spectator*, 14 March 1969.

The introduction of Jo Grant leads to her relationship with the Doctor becoming even more central to the series than might have initially been planned. Furthermore, the arrival of the Master as recurring villain gives the Doctor a specific area of expertise which enhances his importance as an asset to UNIT but also makes him more vulnerable. However, the trajectory towards breaking the dependence on the Brigadier and UNIT is a long one, enduring beyond Jon Pertwee's time in the lead role. UNIT became somewhere that the Doctor knew he had friends, a comfortable berth between perilous adventures. This transition was still in process during the scripting of *The Time Warrior*, with the dialogue between the Doctor and the Brigadier in episode 1 becoming noticeably less antagonistic between the rehearsal script and the camera script.[9]

Terrance Dicks described the return to history for *The Time Warrior* as a 'gimmick', the latest in a series of gimmicks which had included the introduction of the Master, the return of the Daleks, and the return of the first and second Doctors, all as 'hooks' to attract viewers who might have forgotten **Doctor Who** during its six-month absences from BBC One[10]. He didn't mention that **Doctor Who**'s rediscovery of the past, or rather of its freedom to depict imagined versions of historic periods and situations, mirrored **Doctor Who**'s greater awareness of its own longevity as displayed onscreen and off during

---

[9] I am grateful to a private collector for supplying copies of the rehearsal scripts. These were prepared for the 'Outside Rehearsal' period of 16-26 May 1973 when the studio sequences were rehearsed at the BBC Rehearsal Rooms at Acton. The camera scripts are held by the BBC Written Archives Centre.

[10] 'Beginning the End'.

1973. The first episode of *The Time Warrior* was broadcast a few weeks after the publication of a *Radio Times* special commemorating the series' 10th anniversary. This followed publishing initiatives from outside the BBC which were less ephemeral than the annuals and comics. *The Making of Doctor Who* (1972) by Malcolm Hulke and Terrance Dicks, published by Pan Books in their children's imprint Piccolo, explained the production background to the series to a young readership and also retold the Doctor's adventures as far as the opening of *The Sea Devils*, which was being broadcast as the book was published. The following year another new children's imprint, Target, run by Universal-Tandem Publishing, republished three novelisations featuring the first Doctor originally released in the 1960s, with the enthusiastic support of the BBC production team, with new books featuring the third Doctor to follow within weeks of *The Time Warrior* finishing its transmission. The introduction of Sarah Jane Smith as the first new regular character since 1971 thus not only followed an unprecedented gap of nearly three years, but was itself surrounded by paratext of a type which had not existed before. **Doctor Who** was gaining and projecting a sense of itself as historical: its interpreted past now informed the development, promotion and reception of the ongoing series.

Making Sarah Jane Smith's first adventure with the Doctor non-contemporary, and placing the introductory 20th-century framing section at one remove from the familiar UNIT laboratory, emphasised Sarah's independence from the UNIT format. It also was a decisive step in reinventing the Doctor, distinct from his relationship with Jo Grant. While Dicks has the Brigadier mention Jo in thought and speech in the novelisation of the story, she is not referred to in either the rehearsal or camera scripts nor onscreen[11]. In *The Time Warrior* the Doctor is free to improvise again both as problem-solver and as the maker of friendships. While investigating a problem to which he was brought by UNIT, he doesn't have to report back to the Brigadier, there is no Jo to remind him to do so, and he is explicitly shown at the opening of the next story, *Invasion of the Dinosaurs* (1974), displaying indifference over returning to the research centre which was the scene of Linx's kidnappings in *The Time Warrior*. Indeed, that both the Doctor and Sarah are free agents contrasts them with the obsessively dedicated soldier, Linx, and with the medieval humans who are bound to their class and gender roles and to the castles they defend. 'History', here, was a means to demonstrate why **Doctor Who** was still worth watching. It offered an opportunity to pit the Doctor against more monstrous creations of the costume and make-up departments, while relocating the Doctor and newcomer Sarah beyond the established reference points of the third Doctor's era. These were the 'present day', with UNIT; the 'future' seen most recently in *Frontier in Space* (1973); and the 'outer space' discovered there, in *Carnival of Monsters* and in *Planet of the Daleks* (1973). The Doctor's farewell to the Brigadier in episode 1 of *The Time Warrior*, 'a straight line may be the shortest distance between two points, but it is by no means the most interesting,' is through this lens a decisive and mischievous assertion of the Doctor's independence not just from chronology – after all, the Brigadier has no choice but to follow the straight line – but from the ordinary mortality of series formats.

The elements which made up *The Time Warrior* nevertheless needed to be carefully chosen if they were to launch the new season of

[11] Dicks, Terrance, *Doctor Who and the Time Warrior* pp27, 53.

Doctor Who and its new female lead to maximum advantage. Good personal knowledge of an author by the production team was already on public record as a factor in allocating stories to writers. Malcolm Hulke had reportedly been allocated *The Sea Devils* as Barry Letts or Terrance Dicks remembered that he had once been in the navy[12]. One might surmise that Robert Holmes was allocated the launch story for the new companion not only on the precedents of *Spearhead from Space* (1970) which had introduced the third Doctor and the UNIT format, and *Terror of the Autons* (1971), which had introduced Jo Grant, Captain Mike Yates and the Master, but also because he had a varied personal history including roles in the police, and in journalism which implied a capacity for research. Bringing in Holmes' wide experience of life, his ability to build connections between unrelated ideas, and his interest in the topical, ensured that the Middle Ages portrayed by *The Time Warrior* would by necessity draw upon more recent history too.

The three principal creative forces on the serial were thus Dicks, Holmes and Letts. The director, Alan Bromly, was allocated the serial late. Letts had initially intended to direct the serial himself, but was prevented by the need to work on **Moonbase 3** (1973), the series which he and Dicks hoped would release them from long service on **Doctor Who**. Bromly was an experienced director and producer, but his approach was rooted in his experience on the stage and directing for television in the 1950s. His previously expressed wish not to overtire casts was out of step with the pressurised house style of **Doctor Who**, where production stretched the studio environment to

---

[12] Hulke, Malcolm, and Terrance Dicks, *The Making of Doctor Who*, pp74-75.

its limits[13]. Consequently *The Time Warrior* was not as sophisticated a serial in many areas of its execution as had been hoped. Bromly largely left casting to others, including production assistant Marcia Wheeler and also Letts. He was remembered as very resistant to adding shots on location, initially rejecting an offer by a stuntman to improvise a fall from a ladder as it would mean varying a shot list he had already decided upon. Wheeler has remembered his manner as congenial, establishing discipline on set especially over Jon Pertwee, an 'immovable object' triumphing over an 'irresistible force […] His technique was to stand there, say nothing, and say "Right then, we'll do it my way"'[14]. Even then, Wheeler accepted that Bromly was 'not a natural fit' for **Doctor Who**. His unadventurous methods – a tennis ball representing Linx's ship landing in episode 1, or some ill-fitting stock footage depicting the destruction of Irongron's castle in episode 4 – minimalised his creative influence on the serial, and his appearances in the rest of this book are consequently few.

---

[13] For example, when Bromly was producing and often directing the midweek thriller serials for BBC Two in the 1960s he dismissed complaints that his style was too straightforward for a genre which sought complexity, offering that he preferred actors 'to know no more than the episode they are rehearsing, and I ask them […] to play [their characters] for what they seem worth at the time.' (Marjorie Bilbow, 'Who Else is There to Blame But the Director?' *The Stage and Television Today,* 6 May 1965).
[14] *Toby Hadoke's Whosround* 84, 'Marcia Wheeler'.

CHAPTER 1: 'FOR THE ATTENTION OF TERRAN CEDICKS'

Returning to History

Fugitive or Survivor?

Robert Holmes was always at pains to emphasise that it had never been his decision to write a story set in the medieval period. An early DWM described him as having been 'dragged bodily into writing *The Time Warrior* by Terrance Dicks'[15]. This memorably overstated metaphor bears more than a slight relation to his later recollection of the commissioning of *The Time Warrior.*

> 'Terrance Dicks asked me to write an historical adventure for the Doctor. Now this is an area I have always shied away from [...] after some argument, Terrance and I compromised on a story that would be a mix of science fiction and historical fiction.'[16]

The Time Warrior's development was short by comparison with Robert Holmes' previous **Doctor Who** serial. The storyline for *Carnival of Monsters* – then titled 'The Labyrinth' – was commissioned on 1 May 1971 and probably delivered on or by 1 June 1971. The scripts were commissioned on 24 November 1971 and delivered on 23 and 24 December 1971, while the serial itself was recorded between 30 May and 4 July 1972[17]. *The Time Warrior* was commissioned, delivered and produced over a much tighter

---

[15] 'Matrix Data Bank', DWM 70, November 1982.

[16] Comments on Langford, Howard D, 'Moral Symbolism in Doctor Who', *TARDIS* #5:3 & 5:4, 1980.

[17] *Doctor Who: The Complete History* Volume 19, pp58-72.

schedule, after another storyline from Holmes, 'The Automata', had been abandoned. *The Time Warrior* reportedly emerged from a discussion over lunch between Holmes, Dicks and producer Barry Letts in late January or early February 1973; following the approval of the initial storyline, the serial outline was commissioned as 'The Time Fugitive' on 26 February 1973, with a serial commission as 'The Time Survivor' following on 5 March. The scripts were delivered rapidly, episode 1 on 12 March, episodes 2 and 4 on 19 March, and episode 3 on 26 March[18]. The reasons for this hurried delivery are unclear, but perhaps reflect how the long development of *Carnival of Monsters* reflected the refinement of Holmes' own ideas at a time when he had other projects to develop and the **Doctor Who** production office had several other storylines in play. In contrast, *The Time Warrior* was a case of Holmes meeting the challenge of a narrow brief about which he was initially unenthusiastic. Letts and Dicks were working on another series (**Moonbase 3**) as well as **Doctor Who**, and a reliable hand such as Holmes' was needed to launch a new series with a new regular character.

Holmes' initial storyline took the form of a military document, 'For the Attention of Terran Cedicks', written in the character of a Sontaran officer called Hol Mes[19]. This and the two working titles for the serial suggest the evolution of the serial's theme and its principal antagonist. The outline and the transmitted serial differ in several details, but the shape of the story is the same. The main difference is that the storyline document offers a detailed background and characterisation of Linx which could only be implied onscreen. The

---

[18] *The Complete History* Volume 20, pp98-100.
[19] The full storyline appears as 'Interlude VIII' in Richard Molesworth, *Robert Holmes: A Life in Words* pp204-213.

Linx presented by 'Hol Mes' is a hero, a survivor of a major combat in the dying days of a galactic war, who bravely ordered his crew to abandon their damaged ship and took sole responsibility for the fractured vessel. He landed his craft's rear section 'with only one undamaged retro-motor' on the surface of 'an unknown planet, the third in its system in an outer constellation of no strategic value'. Having evaded death in space, Linx uses his ingenuity to make the best of a difficult situation, marshalling the locals of an inferior species in order to create an entire new technology to suit his needs, and when that fails adapting his retro motor and connecting it to his 'osmic-projector' to create a 'time surveyor' which both identified a future era which could provide Linx with a functional workforce and – once a molecular reassembly unit was rigged up – transport them to Linx's era. Much of this appeared in the prologue to *Doctor Who and the Time Warrior*, the only section written by Holmes before he handed the book over to Terrance Dicks to complete[20].

Linx's primary ambition is to return to war. Holmes' Sontaran narrator persona acknowledges that Linx becomes distracted by his obsession with the Doctor and also suffers from 'an efficiency-damaging degree of sub-cultural assimilation' resulting from the period he spends collaborating with Irongron. Nevertheless, this is presented as a side-effect of his determination to expend all possible energies in repairing his spacecraft. Despite his isolation, Mes' Linx remains a combatant even though he is far away from the lines, in a place that does not know an interplanetary conflict is raging around it. He adapts to survive so he can return to the front. His death – in this version, at the hands, or rather arrow, of the Doctor – is an unfortunate side-effect of Linx's 'exceptional valour and devotion to

---

[20] Dicks, *Doctor Who and the Time Warrior*, pp7-16.

the highest ideals of the Sontaran Army Space Service, above and beyond the call of duty.'

One must assume that had Linx not been killed by the Doctor, Hol Mes would have recommended to Terran Cedicks that he receive the first class of the Galactic Hero's Cross, rather than the second mentioned in the concluding paragraph of the document. Nevertheless, 'For the Attention of Terran Cedicks' makes its case well. The title under which the serial was commissioned, 'The Time Survivor', characterises Linx as a combatant who even in utmost adversity is determined to shape and make use of his environment for the benefit of his immediate aims. The meaning, however, was opaque. It's not clear from it whether Linx was a survivor of time, or a survivor within and across time. Nevertheless, 'The Time Survivor' was the name by which the story was known to the BBC Copyright Department until well after it had become *The Time Warrior* to everyone else.

War of the Empires

Robert Holmes had fought in the Second World War in Burma, possibly as one of the Chindits, the special operations units trained for the rigours of jungle warfare beyond the established expectations of the British soldier. His experience of south and south-east Asia influenced his work on **Doctor Who**, demonstrating a fascination with the cultures encountered[21]. Landscapes of gaseous marsh and jungle, echoing those of Burma, appeared in *Carnival of Monsters*, *The Deadly Assassin* (1976) and *The Power of Kroll* (1978). Burma was rich in gas and oil, and competition for natural resources is central to

---

[21] Potter, Ian, **Doctor Who:** *The Black Archive #16: Carnival of Monsters*, pp53-56.

both *Kroll* and *The Caves of Androzani* (1984). *The Time Warrior* owes less to the borrowing of the Burmese landscape than it parodies tales of heroism in hostile theatres of war. Whether he was a member of a Chindit unit, or part of a wider military operation, Holmes would probably have known of the adventures of the Chindit commander, Michael Calvert, who was recruited to the Chindits following an escape from behind enemy lines in Burma which involved him 'strangling a Japanese officer during a naked man-to-man struggle while swimming in the Chindwin, and later [disguising himself] as an Indian woman with a party of Indian refugees'[22].

A friend and colleague of Calvert, Freddie Spencer Chapman, was sent north from Singapore into Malaya on the first reports of a Japanese landing in 1941. He spent the next four years behind enemy lines, often the only British soldier in his party, living in the jungle and working with Chinese Communist guerrillas against the Japanese forces. His account of his experiences, *The Jungle is Neutral*, published in 1949, was titled after his belief that one's environment was neutral; only one's attitude towards it was good or bad and its opportunities and pitfalls should be dealt with as they came. It was an approach which Linx would have understood[23]. The Linx of 'For the Attention of Terran Cedicks' is a copy of neither Calvert nor Chapman. Calvert regarded his killing of a Japanese officer in single combat as akin to murder, and Chapman was inclined to oppose militarism and was happiest extending his and others' understanding

---

[22] Allen, Louis, *Burma: The Longest War 1941-45*, p124. Calvert describes the event in Calvert, Michael, *Fighting Mad*, pp100-03.
[23] 'Freddie Spencer Chapman', *Wikipedia*; 'Chapman, Frederick Spencer (1907–1971), Explorer and Mountaineer', *Oxford Dictionary of National Biography*.

of hazardous environments. Nevertheless, tales of their exploits were used to enhance morale in the field, reviving ideas of British valour and inevitable imperial expansion by military means which, while remote from the reality of the Second World War, remained part of popular culture. Holmes giving Linx the forename Jingo, seen in both 'For the Attention' and the prologue to the novelisation, suggests that embodying propaganda about British imperial superiority in war – 'jingoism' – was innate to his initial conception of Linx[24].

An observation of Chapman's might have contributed to Hol Mes' depiction of Linx's deteriorating psychology:

> '[N]o European can live for a day in an Asiatic country without being recognised as a white man. Therefore, unless a safe area among a friendly people can be found, a European must be perpetually in hiding with obvious bad effects on his health and morale; and if he operates at night or in disguise the strain will be even greater.'[25]

As envisaged in 'For the Attention...' Linx's 'epidermis' did not require the same protection as the 'soft pulpy flesh' of his human hosts. His armour was adopted to hide physical features the humans around

---

[24] Molesworth, *Robert Holmes*, p204; Dicks, *The Time Warrior*, p9. Jingoism originally referred to the ideology of the 'Jingos', a term used for those in 1878 who supported the decision of the British government of Lord Beaconsfield (Benjamin Disraeli) to send a fleet to defend the Ottoman Empire against Russia, but later extended to support for any military action in pursuit of empire. The word comes from the resolute expression used in GW Hunt's music hall song of 1878 'We Don't Want to Fight, but By Jingo, If We Do'.
[25] Chapman, *The Jungle is Neutral*, p10.

him found distressing. Echoing Chapman, the disguise is part of the assimilation which impedes Linx's effectiveness.

While Linx thus has something of the highly skilled and persistent British officer about him, he possesses several levels of ambivalence. The narrative voice in which Holmes wrote 'For the Attention' makes the case for Linx's decoration but admits several failures arising from Linx's mistakes – such as his neglect to take his 'head covering' back to his own time with him after he removed it during a raid on the 20th century – as well as from insurmountable environmental issues which he fails to foresee. There's a sense that for the Sontarans, Linx is already ancient history: his vessel is damaged 'in one of the last actions fought in Galactic War 9', but the 'epic journey' of his four surviving crew members in their life capsule is 'somewhat overshadowed by the outbreak of Galactic War 10'[26].

For all the emphasis lain on Linx as a war hero, and the way his activity recalls the resourcefulness celebrated in coverage of Chapman's career, 'For the Attention' also prompts associations with the *Beyond the Fringe* sketch 'Aftermyth of War'. There, Jonathan Miller's Perkins is ordered to 'lay down [his] life' as 'we need a futile gesture at this stage' to boost morale with a tale of heroics in a so far unsuccessful conflict[27]. Linx's action is probably one among very many competing for recognition in an honours system which assesses, codifies and ranks instances of service to the Sontaran Army Space Service. It's likely that as an army officer in the Second World War, Robert Holmes had to contribute towards such citations with the intention of finding space for fallen comrades in the

[26] Molesworth, *Robert Holmes*, p204.
[27] Bennett, Alan, Peter Cook, Jonathan Miller and Dudley Moore, *The Complete Beyond the Fringe* pp71-72.

extensive military honours system of the British Empire.

On his arrival on Earth, Linx 'adopted a friendly posture' towards the local inhabitants 'in the best traditions of the Sontaran space service' and was 'treated with extreme deference'. Linx follows the precedent of British imperial personalities encountering new peoples. He conforms to a narrative current during Holmes' service in Burma, where benevolent representatives of an advanced empire descend upon primitives, treat them with kindness, awe them with technology, and establish a supposedly mutually beneficial partnership. Indeed, the manner in which the Japanese had patronised the Burmese independence movement, especially in rural districts with little economic or colonial infrastructure, could be understood in similar terms[28]. It still hung over Britain's relations with her current and former colonies during the early 1970s, rhetoric in its tradition having been used to justify the ill-conceived and ill-fated Federation of Rhodesia and Nyasaland, dissolved in 1963, as well as ongoing white minority regimes in Rhodesia (one of the federation's three successor states) and South Africa. The British Empire was not a monolith of governmental, military or commercial models, and benevolent paternalism was not the only narrative of British imperialism echoed in Linx's conduct, either in 'For the Attention' or in later iterations of *The Time Warrior*. Linx's aggressive pursuit of human and material resources had been the method of British colonists since the days of John Smith in Virginia in the early 17th century. Linx explores Earth (or specifically one corner of it) in time, where Smith explored North American space.

---

[28] Allen, Louis, *Burma*, pp22-24.

A Bunch of Gooks

A correlation with European settlement in North America, and the United States which rose from it, might be of further relevance because Linx's language and culture in 'For the Attention' caricature American military slang. Linx describes Irongron and his band, when he first meets them, as 'a bunch of gooks'. 'Gook' is a word of contested origin, perhaps owing something to the term 'gugoos' with which American soldiers occupying the Philippines from 1898 onwards demeaned the indigenous people. From about 1947 'gook' in English became largely used as a derogatory term for East Asians encountered by US forces, perhaps deriving from the Korean words for country ('guk') and for America ('miguk')[29]. By the late 1960s it was appearing in journalism critical of the conduct of the USA in the Vietnam War. As one contributor to *The New Republic* wrote in 1969:

> 'It was then [the arrival of US forces in Korea in 1950] that the fact that Americans should never be required to fight among or for or against people whom they call "gooks" began to be documented in blood [...] Here I testify from knowledge of myself. On an April afternoon, in 1966 [...] I noticed [...] a bowlegged and very small Vietnamese man running [...] I assumed that he was running to tell the Vietcong of our presence and I thought to myself that somebody ought to shoot the goddamned gook.'[30]

The term was dismissive and fatally dehumanising of inhabitants of

---

[29] 'gook, n.', *OED Online*; Turse, Nick, *Kill Anything That Moves*, pp49-51.
[30] Osborne, John, 'Death to Gooks', *The New Republic,* 13 December 1969.

Korea and Vietnam in the minds of Americans fighting with them; Linx's use of it was a guide to the reader (one intended recipient in particular, Terrance Dicks) that that for all his outer benevolence towards Irongron and his henchmen, Linx regarded them as inferior and expendable. Indeed, Linx's confidence in Sontaran technological as well as military superiority echoes the assumptions made first by the French in their war to restore their colonial mastery in Vietnam, and then by the Americans in their war against the Communist government of North Vietnam: that military and cultural supremacy naturally fell to a philosophically, scientifically and materially enlightened society which Vietnam, 'a nation of peasants with bicycles', could not be[31].

While the viewer – and the dominant assumptions of the broadcast version – might be as confident as Linx of their superiority to the medieval combatants and their technology of armourers and blacksmiths, bows and arrows, Holmes' storyline is not. It can even be argued that almost everything achieved by the Doctor and Sarah could have been managed by a knowledgeable inhabitant of the period. A scene in the rehearsal script for episode 1, excised by the time of recording, established that Irongron was immune to Linx's technologically-driven hypnotism. Sarah's first intervention forestalled an assassination attempt on Irongron which, had it been successful, might have deprived Linx of shelter as well as a reliable ally. The only problem for the medieval inhabitants would have been what to do with the enslaved scientists, Linx's ship and his osmic projector, which needs the Doctor's insight to enable the safe return home of the prisoners.

---

[31] Gibson, James William, *The Perfect War*, p17.

Linx's dismissal of Irongron and his band as 'gooks' also encourages assumptions about Linx's attitude to his environment as a theatre of war. Despite the references to Sontaran army best practice and to military honour throughout 'For the Attention', the values of the Sontarans are those of what has since been termed the 'doctrine of atrocity' pursued by members of US forces in Vietnam. Incidents such as the My Lai massacre, when American soldiers killed the inhabitants of a non-combatant Vietnamese village, were not isolated. Awareness of American military action against civilians in Vietnam was high in early 1970s Anglophone culture. In 1971 *The New York Times* listed 33 recent books which had considered American atrocities in Vietnam[32]. Followers of the war in the British press could build a picture of the US army as drug-addicted or mutinous, perpetrating 'the ruthless murder of a nation'[33].

The conduct of the USA in Vietnam was used to make British readers feel more civilised than their American cousins, as young American immigrants to the United Kingdom cited their disenchantment with the war as one of their reasons for emigrating, while the Union of American Exiles in Britain found some politicians sympathetic when they sought help for those who were living clandestinely in Britain to avoid being drafted into the US Army, even though a fundraising

---

[32] Turse, *Kill Anything That Moves*, pp2-4, 101-102, 239-40, citing Sheehan, Neil, 'Should We Have War Crime Trials?', *The New York Times*, 28 March 1971.

[33] '30,000 Vietnam Men on Heroin', *Daily Mirror*, 30 April 1971; 'Vietnam Revolt', *Daily Mirror*, 13 April 1972; 'Vietnam: Why the Silence?', *Daily Mirror*, 28 December 1972.

appeal had little success[34]. The writer Cameron Duodu, a Ghanaian citizen visiting the USA as a guest of the State Department, told readers of British newspaper *The Guardian* that the USA's exposure of children to 'violence and hatred' led to the glamorisation of destruction, whether in campus shootings 'or at the controls of a B-52 dishing out napalm in Vietnam'[35].

Duodu pinpoints a concern or perception non-Americans might have shared of American desensitisation towards violence, and which Robert Holmes could employ. When Holmes has Linx talk of Irongron 'pow-zap[ping] the stinking little creeps', he has him using terms borrowed from the 'sound effects' of comic strips popularised (and satirised) by the **Batman** television series. Holmes thus uses the language of American low culture to illustrate Linx's entertainment by the violence which he encourages human beings to inflict upon each other. While couched in the language of military honour, Linx's own words allude succinctly to the violence inflicted on the Vietnamese with little or no military justification, at best incomprehensible to those following the conflict from other countries, as well the cultural values which the prejudices of British observers might suspect underpinned American warfare.

Robert Holmes told later interviewers that the militarism of the Sontarans was inspired by 'reading, or trying to read, *Clausewitz on War*'[36]. *On War* by Carl Friedrich Gottfried von Clausewitz (1780-

---

[34] Daley, Janet, *The Guardian*, 1 January 1968; 'Sanctuary Sought for US Evaders', *The Guardian*, 1 July 1969; '"Asylum" Plea for Deserters', *The Guardian*, 16 October 1970.
[35] Duodu, Cameron, 'Land of Black Baddies', *The Guardian*, 7 December 1968.
[36] Comments on Langford, 'Moral Symbolism in Doctor Who', p24.

1831), was first published in German in 1832. In 1973, its most easily available version was the Pelican Classics edition, published in 1968, which in turn abridged a revised English translation of 1908. Holmes peppers 'For the Attention' with cross-references, principally to invented military sources. 'The War Manual, Vol. VII, Feasibility of Further Galactic Conquest' is most obviously spoofing Clausewitz (*On War* is divided into six books).

Holmes later recalled *On War* as 'some heavy tome [...] it was terribly Teutonic and all about the Fatherland and so on.'[37] 'Teutonic'' and 'Fatherland' suggest Germany – the Germany as an enemy of the UK experienced in the First and Second World Wars – as a further inspiration for Linx. However, there is very little in the storyline or in the serial as produced which displays a debt to precedents of specifically German conduct in 20th-century warfare. The use of forced labour, poorly fed, features in *The Time Warrior* from first conception. The rehearsal script for episode 1 describes Linx's prisoners as 'shabby, dirty and emaciated'. Later, they begin to collapse from malnutrition. Both child and adult viewer might have made a connection with inmates in German concentration camps. Closer to Holmes' experience, though, was the treatment of British prisoners of war by the Japanese army during the Second World War. The brutality of the Japanese regime towards enemy internees, their lack of nourishment and insanitary conditions, were already part of popular culture through novels and films such as *The Bridge on the*

---

[37] Marson, Richard. and Mulkern, Patrick, 'The Pertwee Years', *Doctor Who Magazine* (DWM) Winter Special 1985.

River Kwai and *King Rat*[38]. While perhaps not known to the younger section of the audience who were **Doctor Who**'s main target, such allusions would have been recognised on broadcast by a good proportion of the '60% adult' audience referred to by Barry Letts in interviews during his producership and subsequently. The Sontarans' dedication to war draws from the memory of imperial Japan as an expansionist and insensitive war machine.

The Linx of 'For the Attention' embodies other 1970s British cultural assumptions about Japan. The time fugitives and time survivors of the post-war decades were the Japanese soldiers who refused to surrender, for a variety of motives, and behaved as combatants until killed or captured. One 'straggler', Shoichi Yokoi, was captured on Guam in 1972, while another, Kinshichi Kozuka, was killed in the Philippines. They were the first discovered since 1960. Their existence raised the possibility that others survived, either removed from society as Yokoi and Kozuka had lived, or who had integrated with a host community and shared their skills. This turned out to be the course taken by two Japanese soldiers in Malaya, Shigeyuki Hashimoto and Kiyoaki Tanaka, who only returned to Japan in 1990 after spending decades with the Communist guerrilla forces fighting first Britain and then the independent state of Malaysia[39]. The Sontaran army of 'For the Attention' can be interpreted as a projection of the Japanese Empire these soldiers believed in – the undefeatable focus of unquestioned devotion, pursuing military

---

[38] Boulle, Pierre, *Le Pont de la Rivière Kwaï* (1952); *The Bridge on the River Kwai*, dir David Lean (1957); Clavell, James, *King Rat* (1962); *King Rat,* dir Bryan Forbes (1965).

[39] 'WWII Die-hards Receive Cool Greeting in Japan', *Chicago Tribune*, 15 January 1990.

expansion against 'vipers', whether of Rutan or the European powers.

Toad Face

The influence of the Far East continued to shape *The Time Warrior* at script stage. It's not clear from 'For the Attention' what sort of Earth creatures the Sontarans most resemble, only that their body has more natural outward protection than human beings, and that they are contrasted with the 'hominids' who are the dominant species on Earth. The rehearsal script for episode 1 describes Linx removing his helmet to reveal a 'hideous toad-like alien face'. The scene was written up after the fact; by the time rehearsals at Acton began on 16 May 1973, the sequence had already been filmed at Peckforton Castle. However, the toad comparison carries through into dialogue. The rehearsal script for episode 3 sees Irongron call Linx a 'little toad' (twice), 'toad-face', 'good toadface', 'good toad' but also a 'little owl'; in episode 4 he is 'a scabby-faced stoat', 'you foul beetle, you cockroach, you bed louse', but also (when good relations between the two have been restored) 'old toad' and again 'good toad' when he expresses his disbelief that Linx will leave. In contrasting himself with Linx, Irongron says he is 'not an owl', but then after Linx leaves describes him as 'a toad at heart'. He also mocks Linx for having 'great feet' which he couldn't imagine on a scaling ladder.

The overall impression is that Linx largely resembles a toad but has some features which are bird-like or rodent-like. The qualities are those a writer might attribute to a species adapted to amphibious and airborne warfare, which characterised much of the Second World War in south-east Asia. There, the Indian and Pacific oceans were theatres of war and adaptability to both sea and land was crucial. The same was true in the Vietnam War. The largely amphibious, owl-like, nocturnal Linx, whether by accident or design, is a projection of what evolution, if given a free if somewhat literal hand, might make of the imperial powers competing in South East Asia. In March 1973, while Holmes was writing the story, US President Richard M Nixon suspended the withdrawal of American troops from Vietnam. There seemed every possibility that the war would drag on despite Nixon's promise to end American involvement.

As Irongron calls Linx a 'little toad', the Doctor describes the Sontaran to Sarah as 'nasty, brutish and short'[40]. This quotation comes to *The Time Warrior* from *Leviathan* (1651), the principal work of the 17th-century English political philosopher Thomas Hobbes, specifically Part One, Chapter 13, 'Of the Natural Condition of Mankind as Concerning their Felicity and Misery'. Within this chapter Hobbes discussed competition between men, that war arose when there was no 'common power' to overawe them and keep the peace, and in a state of war life was 'solitary, poor, nasty, brutish, and short'. On the one hand, this is a summary of the situation of the story, for with the king absent with most of the fighting men – those troops who are 'all at the wars', as Irongron tells Linx – there is nothing to stop Irongron overthrowing Sir Edward but discipline, manpower, weaponry and opportunity. In its immediate context, though, the script is confirming that Linx is of smaller than average (male) human height. To the British forces of the Far East campaign, one nickname for the Japanese was the 'little men', a description rooted in decades of nervous clutching at notions of white European superiority over

----

[40] Part Three. (Unless otherwise indicated, all episodic quotes are from *The Time Warrior*.)

complex Asian civilisations[41]. 'Warlike' was an adjective routinely attributed to the Japanese by the early 20th century, and little opportunity is lost by 'For the Attention' or the script of *The Time Warrior* to emphasise the Sontarans' militarism.

There is evidence for Japanese influence on how the script envisaged Linx's appearance. In episode 1, Linx's entry into scene 12 – his return to Irongron's great hall, where he volunteers to take over the interrogation of Sir Edward's messenger Eric – is 'A squat broad figure encased in black armour appears in the door' – and while Irongron (at least, in the rehearsal script) hails him as 'A parfait gentil knight!' the description might suggest less Geoffrey Chaucer's Knight from *The Canterbury Tales* (c1400) than a Samurai warrior. The first Japanese armour known to have reached Britain was the suit presented to James VI and I in 1613 on behalf of Shogun Tokugawa Hidetada[42]. This largely dark red and black suit had been restored for display at the Tower of London in 1972, although it does not seem to have attracted media attention. Another, darker suit is held by the British Museum. If the script is drawing on the impression these made, that impression is immediately contrasted with Irongron's (probable) anticipation of Chaucer (who wrote after the likely date of the serial's setting) to set up the culture clash between Irongron and Linx and their differing attitudes to war, hospitality and service. The past is contested between Irongron's acquisitive, casual basis for

---

[41] This stereotype was present in both peace and war. Japanese staff at the Japan-British exhibition of 1910 were described in the *Daily Express*, 29 April 1910, as 'the three hundred [...] little Japanese men who are working for the honour of Japan at Shepherd's Bush' See Mutsu, Hirokichi, ed, *The British Press and the Japan-British Exhibition of 1910* p47.

[42] 'Armour – Domaru' (1570), *Royal Armouries* website.

military expeditions and Linx's highly theoretical and dogmatic militarism. In this sense *The Time Warrior* recollects British myths about imperial expansion – acquiring Empire in 'a fit of absence of mind' while concentrating on trade and on European rather than world diplomacy – contrasted with the systematic conquest associated with Britain's imperial enemies, especially her rivals from the late 19th century onwards, Germany and Japan[43].

The Spaceman in the Window

Robert Holmes' career in magazine journalism in the 1950s had largely been spent on the illustrated news feature and fiction weekly *John Bull*. He contributed five stories under his own name between 1956 and 1958, and for at least some of that period and perhaps beyond was one of its editorial staff.

John Bull had roots in English patriotism. It took its name from the character of John Bull invented as an allegory of England by John Arbuthnot for his satire *The History of John Bull* in 1712, but which evolved through the late 18th and 19th centuries into a symbol of the unsophisticated Englishman (or Briton), put upon by complexity and corruption in the state and the economy but whose plainspoken questions would at some point in time win through[44]. The periodical

---

[43] The oft-quoted 'fit of absence of mind' stems from Seeley, JC, *The Expansion of England* (1883), p9. Seeley's work was an early exploration of the tensions between the 19th-century conception of the nation state and empire, between the ideals of 'Liberty! Democracy!' and control of other countries by another, and the absence of a world outlook in most people in Great Britain which failed to appreciate the many facets of empire.

[44] Taylor, Miles, 'Bull, John (fl. 1712-)', *Oxford Dictionary of National Biography*.

John Bull was founded in 1906 to promote its editor and first proprietor, Horatio Bottomley, through identifying him with the cause of the 'little man' and thus with Bull[45]. Bottomley pursued a sensationalist agenda then rare in the British press, which at the outbreak of the First World War became a 'venomous chauvinism' directed against German immigrants to Britain[46]. *John Bull* campaigned aggressively for men to volunteer for battle.

Bottomley was a popular celebrity whose influence on the British self-image was substantial in the early 20th century, but his luck ran out. Early in the magazine's career he had been relieved of the proprietorship of *John Bull* by its printers, Odhams, and in 1921 was dismissed from the editorship. In 1922 he was sent to prison for fraud. Odhams still published *John Bull* when Holmes was on its staff; Bottomley remained a legend of Fleet Street and working in his shadow, even at three or four decades' distance, was bound to contribute towards the scepticism towards imperialism and jingoistic patriotism demonstrated in Holmes' writing.

In the 1950s *John Bull* appears to have avoided controversy. Several of the contributors to *John Bull* would become recognisable to the television audiences of the 1960s and 1970s – Wilfred Greatorex, NJ Crisp, Bill Strutton, and Holmes' near-namesake Robert Holles[47].

---

[45] Cox, Howard, and Simon Mowatt, *Revolutions from Grub Street: A History of Magazine Publishing in Britain*, pp56-58.

[46] Morris, AJA, 'Bottomley, Horatio William (1860–1933), Journalist and Swindler'. *Oxford Dictionary of National Biography*.

[47] Greatorex's television credits include creating corporate dramas **The Plane Makers** (1963-65) and **The Power Game** (1965-69) and near-future dystopia **1990** (1977-78). NJ Crisp co-created **The Brothers** (1972-76) as well as writing multiple episodes of series including **Secret Army** (1977-79); Bill Strutton is probably best known

Others became or were already established in other areas, such as Agatha Christie, Doris Lessing and Nevil Shute. Its cover illustrations tended to celebrate a comfortable domesticity in which traditional gender and generational roles were confirmed. Sometimes family members were illustrated taking advantage of modern gadgets, especially the television, whose stars (including David Attenborough, Eamonn Andrews and Jimmy Edwards) and schedules took up a growing amount of *John Bull*'s attention.

One cover illustration might anticipate *The Time Warrior*. 'For the Attention' describes how Linx clad himself in human armour in order to 'conceal his differing physiognomy'. The rehearsal script for episode 1 removes this potential problem, explaining that 'Sontaran space armour' is 'not unlike a gleaming, sophisticated version of the knight's armour of the period'. The painting by Kenneth John Petts on the cover of *John Bull* dated week ending 9 November 1957 showed a couple examining pottery ornaments inside a shop in a historic town. Half-timbered buildings frame a church tower and hoardings which perhaps shelter the site of a new construction. In front and to the couple's right is a small boy in a red school uniform. He is not looking at the pottery but at the suit of armour in the foreground which looms from the couple's left. Text inside the magazine explains that:

> 'Junior [...] seem[s] to think that that suit of armour has conversion possibilities as a spaceman's suit. Maybe there's something in that, too, since a knight's armour weighed less

to readers of this book for writing **Doctor Who** serial *The Web Planet* (1965) and its novelisation *Doctor Who and the Zarbi*; Robert Holles wrote several television plays, often about military life.

than a First World War soldier's kit.'[48]

Perhaps this cover lurked somewhere in Robert Holmes' memory and pointed the way to *The Time Warrior*'s couching of modernity in medievalism.

[48] *John Bull*, 9 November 1957.

CHAPTER 2: MEDIEVAL LINKS

The Time Warrior's Sense of History

A great deal of the dynamism of *The Time Warrior* – at least for an adult audience and perhaps also for the performers – stems from its use of contemporary and near-contemporary points of comparison for the characters and situations in the story. However, its priority was to present a convincing medieval setting for the Doctor's latest adventure. It achieved this through the adaptation of signs representing the Middle Ages already familiar to sections of its audience.

Sci-Attica

A tension had existed in **Doctor Who** between realistic and romantic modes of storytelling from its inception. The writers' guide used throughout the first Doctor's tenure provided a generic location for **Doctor Who** between negatives – it was neither fantasy nor science fiction. Its aspiration for realism was part of how early **Doctor Who** sought to reflect the mission of its co-creator Sydney Newman. It is a concern, an anxiety, expressed in the agonised conversation of memos between the first serial's writer, Anthony Coburn, and its story editor, David Whitaker, over whether the cavemen in *An Unearthly Child* (1963) should talk, and second story director Richard Martin's notes attempting to rationalise the dimensional transcendence of the TARDIS[49]. The imaginative and logistical limitations of making a weekly serial on a limited budget which varied its settings frequently while aiming at a wide audience

---

[49] Howe, David J, Mark Stammers and Stephen James Walker, *Doctor Who: The Handbook – The First Doctor*, pp225-26.

precluded innovations, which denied viewers the steadying handrail of convention. The complaint relayed to the production team in 1964 from the BBC's director of television, Kenneth Adam, that there were 'so many refugees from Attica or, if you prefer, the Eisteddfod wandering around' during *The Keys of Marinus* (1964), recognised the problems **Doctor Who** had in finding an acceptable visual grammar for the otherworldly when it had by necessity to draw on human societies of present and past for inspiration[50].

An argument can be made that for **Doctor Who's** first decade, the majority of alien life forms and societies can be categorised using the labels atomic, bestial or classical. The Daleks and Cybermen are both creatures of the atomic age, a post-Second World War society which is concerned that, while it possesses unprecedented capacity for destruction, it does not know how it can reassemble a society from the ruins of that destruction, and also fears the end result. The Ice Warriors meanwhile subsume their electronic implants into a body which does not look robotic but instead like the offspring of a crocodile and a tortoise, but standing upright and with fur, a hybrid of two branches of the animal kingdom. Other societies tend to be characterised by philosophy: the technologically-enforced communitarianism of Marinus, the self-congratulatory parasitism of the Elders in *The Savages* (1966), the passivity of the Dulcians and violence of their Dominator foes (*The Dominators*, 1968). These all echo schoolroom contrasts between the supposed characters of the different city-states in ancient Greece. These stereotypes themselves derived from classical sources rediscovered in western Europe during the Renaissance and which shaped the way political actors and

---

[50] Kenneth Adam to Stuart Hood (controller of programmes, television), 28 April 1964, BBC WAC T5/647/1.

47

polities presented themselves.

The history painting reached Great Britain during the 17th century, presenting kings, generals and statesmen as generals or orators from an imagined classical world, clad in togas, sheets or else naked. The influence on costumes for *The Keys of Marinus* or *The Dominators* is plain, in different ways, though Robin Phillips' Altos in *Marinus* is probably the closest one gets to the short-skirted Hellenic hero outside those stories actually set in classical history or mythology. Another exception is the Hellenic influence on the costumes of the people of Peladon in *The Curse of Peladon* (1972), not so much the Renaissance garb of the king and nobility, but the soldiery. The costumes of the king's guards in particular have less to do with representations of medieval Europe than they have with the soldiers seen on Greek vases. They share in an established tradition of costuming for television productions set in the ancient world which included not only **Doctor Who**'s *The Myth Makers* (1965), but more importantly Rudolph Cartier's BBC production of Terence Rattigan's *Adventure Story* (1961) with Sean Connery as Alexander the Great and William Russell as Hephaestion, or Philip Mackie's series for Granada, **The Caesars** (1969).

The Rise of the Gothic

Classicism was a dominant tradition in education, in culture and in politics for several centuries in Britain. Children, especially boys, learned Latin and Ancient Greek at school, studied the works of writers in those languages from the ancient world, and were encouraged to understand their own society in terms of the Greek republics and kingdoms and the Roman republic and empire. It's unsurprising that it should have shaped dramatic conventions on television, nor specifically those of **Doctor Who**. Aside from *The Romans* (1965) itself, perhaps the **Doctor Who** story of the 1960s which most obviously draws on received views about classical history is *The Dominators,* where concerns about 20th-century warfare and British society's memories of it are interpreted in terms of the senatorial government and cosseted aristocracy of the Dulcians, with their largely Latinate society, ripe for destruction by the vigorous and warlike Dominators, who nevertheless have nothing culturally to offer beyond being better at war than the Dulcians.

The rise of the Gothic aesthetic in British culture reacted against the classical artistic tradition and the ideas about society which underpinned it. This inevitably involved a substantial degree of invention, conscious and unconscious. From the early 17th century, critics of untrammelled monarchy in England imagined the Gothic peoples (probably from the Danube, speaking a Germanic language or languages) who had invaded and overthrown the Roman Empire in the west in the fifth century as confederations of free peoples who followed a 'Gothic' constitution of elective rather than autocratic government[51].

In early 18th-century Britain, unified and largely at peace following a century of unrest and revolution, the Gothic offered an ideology for newly-emerged political dynasties such as the Temple and Grenville families, who from the 1730s developed a series of Gothic allusions in landscape and buildings at their gardens at Stowe, Buckinghamshire, asserting that they were the real custodians of the

---

[51] There are many sources on the development of the Gothic, but Groom, Nick, *The Gothic: A Very Short Introduction* is both wide-ranging and succinct.

Gothic tradition in England[52].

Helmets and Ghosts: The Castle of Otranto

This dynastic proprietorship was challenged and overturned by a political and literary rival who had a greater intellectual and material appreciation of what the Gothic could mean. Horace Walpole was the youngest son of Sir Robert Walpole (traditionally regarded as Britain's first prime minister) and devoted his substantial inheritance to the extension and beautification of his home at Strawberry Hill, Twickenham, west of London. His time was spent collecting books and works of art, and writing. He conducted the most extensive political and literary correspondence of 18th-century Britain and composed political propaganda for several governments as well as history and fiction. Walpole's Middle Ages were not a period of enhanced liberty but the home of superstition and repression. However, he also saw in them space for imaginative expression which was itself repressed by the 'polite and commercial' rationalist Britons[53]. In *The Castle of Otranto* (1764), he invented the Gothic novel, though it took time to find its imitators[54].

In the first edition of the book, Walpole affects to present his novel as a translation from an Italian source printed in Naples in 1529. His

---

[52] Gerrard, Christine, *The Patriot Opposition to Walpole: Politics, Poetry and National Myth 1725-174*) remains the best guide to this movement. Kilburn, Matthew, 'Cobham's Cubs (act 1734–1747)', *Oxford Dictionary of National Biography* is, I hope, a reliable concise view.

[53] Blackstone, William *Commentaries on the Laws of England*, vol 3, p326.

[54] Walpole, Horace, *The Castle of Otranto*, ed WS Lewis, with a new introduction and notes by E.J. Clery, ppx-xi.

preface invites his readers to see through his deception: for example, with the anachronism of the Spanish personal names used for servants in the novel with the time and place in which it purported to have been originally composed. The vagueness of *The Castle of Otranto*'s historical setting – sometime in the Middle Ages, in the age of castles so probably following the Norman conquest of Sicily in the 11th century, but with other clues implying the 13th or 14th centuries or later – anticipates the similar ambiguity over period seen in *The Time Warrior.*

Several features of *The Time Warrior* owe something to Walpole's story, which itself drew on established motifs known to Walpole from earlier works. The castle of Otranto itself is in the possession of a usurper, Manfred, albeit in this case the grandson of the man who stole it from its rightful possessor. The way through to the main part of the plot is signed by an apparition and by finding a way round an impenetrable trapdoor (in this case a literal one rather than a time corridor). A helmet conceals for a time the identity of a morally ambivalent figure – Frederic, marquis of Vicenza, father of the novel's heroine Isabella – who has the opportunity to choose well, but does not. The friar, Jerome (also a lord) whose knowledge and judgement provide a resolution to the mystery is at times mistrusted by all sides. An object which falls from space early in the novel contributes towards an explosion at the conclusion which destroys the disputed castle.

The Time Warrior was not the first **Doctor Who** serial to draw on Gothic material in the manner of *The Castle of Otranto*. An obvious example is *The Crusade* (1965), where David Whitaker has the TARDIS materialise in a wood outside Jaffa. A wood outside Jaffa (called Joppa in *Otranto*) is the location of the hermit's retreat where

Frederic is charged with restoring Otranto to its rightful heir (whom he assumes to be himself). The fourth episode of *The Chase*, 'Journey into Terror', demonstrated Terry Nation's fondness for the Gothic as mediated through horror cinema. This was clearest in an early draft, where the mundane revelation that the TARDIS crew were interacting with robot versions of Dracula and Frankenstein's Monster in a haunted house exhibit at the Festival of Ghana in 1996 did not appear, and the Doctor's pronouncement that the TARDIS had materialised in a world formed from 'the dark recesses of the human minds' was to be taken literally[55].

The insistence on the primacy of science and rationality over superstition in *The Dæmons* (1971) might preclude it being considered truly Gothic in spirit as a **Doctor Who** story; despite the first episode suggesting the subversion of rational enquiry by supernatural forces, the theatricality of the Master (whose high priest outfit recalls that worn by Boris Karloff as Hjalmar Poelzig in the Universal horror film *The Black Cat* (1934)) rapidly recodes the supernatural as a performance to obscure the explicability of Dæmonic science. Also rendered marginal by story development is the planet Peladon. It is introduced with Gothic trappings, recognised in its conventional description as a medieval society making an awkward transition into membership of the Galactic Federation[56]. This suggested that the story would draw on medieval

---

[55] Pixley, Andrew, 'Frankenstein Vs the Daleks', *The Essential Doctor Who issue 12: Time Travel*.

[56] For example, see 'The Gloomy Medieval-Gothic Planet/Kingdom of Peladon', Christopher Bahn, '**Doctor Who** (Classic): *The Curse of Peladon*', *AV/TV Club*, 1 April 2012; 'The Residents of Peladon Totally Resemble Middle Age Humans', Steve Ashfield, '**Doctor Who**: The Curse of Peladon', *Television Heaven*, May 2014.

models or later designs and stories inspired by the Middle Ages. The language of supernatural intervention in which the death of Chancellor Torbis is couched, and the end of episode 1 in which Aggedor's statue falls towards the delegates, echoes the plummeting helmet which kills Conrad, Manfred's son and heir, early in *The Castle of Otranto*. However, the Gothic preoccupations of contested identity, though present in the half-Terran King Peladon, are underplayed in favour of diplomatic intrigue owing more to 20th-century world war and Cold War models, while the language of 'barbarism' and civilisation also present in *The Curse of Peladon* suggests the influence of both classical and British imperialist concerns[57].

The Time Warrior's use of elements harvested from Gothic literature was probably the most thoroughgoing seen in **Doctor Who** at that point. Robert Holmes was as much a self-conscious architect of effect and exploiter of culturally current images and ideas as Horace Walpole. If his (young) audience were unfamiliar with them, then the inclusions of signs borrowed from earlier books and films was an introduction to a tradition they could explore later. Holmes seems always to have been wary of educational material in **Doctor Who** – 'I have a feeling that **Doctor Who** was originally developed by Auntie as a format for making history interesting for children; fortunately, the fantasy side soon took over'[58]; but that fantasy itself was rich with items of remembered creative works, comparable to the fragments of story and old ways of seeing which fascinated Walpole.

---

[57] 'We come to help your people, to raise them from barbarism.' (Alpha Centauri, *The Curse of Peladon*, Episode 2).
[58] Holmes commenting on Langford, quoted in Langford, 'Moral Symbolism in Doctor Who', p24.

The imperative for the 20th-century writer for hire, as for the 18th-century gentleman author, was to make from this something of the present moment, where his characters 'think, speak and act' as ordinary people 'would do in extraordinary positions' rather than themselves become divorced from their 'natural' behaviour by the prevalent supernatural[59].

Walpole attributed the origins of *The Castle of Otranto* to a dream of a gigantic hand in armour, holding a bannister on a stairway. It's tempting to see this as directly anticipating the spectral appearance of the armoured Linx on the research centre stairway in *The Time Warrior* episode 1. By *The Time Warrior* Holmes' **Doctor Who** stories had acquired qualities of a series of vivid dreams, where some dreamers were more conscious of their predicament than others. As early as *Spearhead from Space*, the Doctor breaks the sleepwalker-like conditioning of Hibbert, and in *Carnival of Monsters* the Doctor and Jo are frustrated by the manipulation of the memories of the inhabitants of the SS *Bernice. The Time Warrior* has its hypnotised scientists and its time-travelling humans who take time to accept that they are in the Middle Ages, but even then don't abandon their 20th-century ways.

Henry Fuseli and Earth's Dark Legends

Another striking Gothic source for *The Time Warrior* invokes the dream as a plane of existence with parallels and consequences in the waking world. This is the painting 'The Nightmare', exhibited in 1782 by Henry Fuseli (1741-1825). Fuseli, born Johann Heinrch Füssli in Zürich, Switzerland, had been influenced by the German 'Sturm und Drang' – 'storm and urge' – artistic movement which in turn had

---

[59] Walpole, *The Castle of Otranto*, p10.

looked to some of the same precedents as Horace Walpole. 'The Nightmare' expresses Fuseli's futile infatuation with Anna Landolt, the niece of his friend and mentor Johann Caspar Lavater. Fuseli notoriously expressed his passion for Landolt in the description of a dream union of repressed eroticism: 'Last night I had her in bed with me [...] fused her body and her soul together with my own [...] Anyone who touches her now commits adultery and incest! She is mine and I am hers.'[60] In 'The Nightmare' the figure of a young woman based on Landolt is seen recumbent on a bed while a stunted demonic figure of brownish skin, wide grimacing mouth and suggestion of beard crouches over her. A manic horse looks on from behind a curtain. In the painting Fuseli perhaps condemned his own feelings for Landolt, which he is believed never to have declared to her.

No description of Linx in the script for *The Time Warrior* suggests a connection with the demon of 'The Nightmare'. James Acheson, costume designer on *The Time Warrior*, commented (when discussing the Gell guards in *The Three Doctors*) that 'often a literary or mental idea of what a monster ought to look like is hugely impractical [...] often one has to throw out an author's concept.'[61] The sparse and general references to toads and owls were hints by Holmes rather than requirements. John Friedlander, visual effects designer on the story, realised Linx's mask by playing to his own strengths, merging prosthetics and an actor's face following the precedent of the Ogrons and the Draconians. The central concept, described by Acheson as 'a very silly idea that [...] when he took the helmet off the head would be almost the same size and shape', didn't

---

[60] Mason, EC, *The Mind of Henry Fuseli*, p155.
[61] 'James Acheson Interview', *The Frame* 4, November 1987.

prevent other influences. The depression in Linx's brow above his nose and the suggestion of a beard could well be nods to Fuseli's first version of 'The Nightmare' and to the engraving of 1783 after Fuseli by T Burke[62]. Terrance Dicks' novelisation also encourages a comparison. The narrator describes Linx's unmasked features thus:

> 'The face beneath was something out of a nightmare. The head was huge and round, emerging directly from the massive shoulders. The hairless skull was greenish-brown in colour, the eyes small and red. The little nose was a pig-like snout, the mouth long and lipless. It was a face from one of Earth's dark legends, the face of a goblin or a troll.'[63]

It was not the first time a figure resembling the demon from 'The Nightmare' had appeared in a Robert Holmes **Doctor Who** story. The troll doll in *Terror of the Autons* which murders the elder Farrell also bears a resemblance to Fuseli's demon. Both stories were made during a period when Fuseli was being reassessed by art historians. Critics earlier in the 20th century had been divided between seeing Fuseli as a forerunner of the Surrealists or not to be taken seriously at all[64]. In the run-up to the making of *The Time Warrior*, 'The Nightmare' was reproduced in *The Times* on 18 January 1973 in an article reviewing two books about Fuseli, one of which was also

---

[62] Powell, Nicolas, *Fuseli: The Nightmare*, p14.

[63] Dicks, *The Time Warrior*, p60. Dicks takes the analogy even further in *Doctor Who and the Invasion of Time*, p101, where he describes the unmasked Sontaran as having 'a face from some ancient nightmare.'

[64] Powell, *Fuseli: The Nightmare*, p95.

reviewed in *The Spectator* in March[65]. Fuseli was also represented that year in an exhibition at the Royal Academy, London, *English Drawings and Watercolours 1550-1850*[66]. While not the centre of a major rediscovery, he was enjoying more currency than usual at the time *The Time Warrior* was conceived.

There are qualifications to the analogy. The principal female character in *The Time Warrior*, Sarah Jane Smith, has very little directly to do with Linx. It was left to his successor, Styre, to carry the parallels forward in *The Sontaran Experiment* (1975) by capturing Sarah and inducing nightmarish hallucinations which appear to turn her fears into actuality – perhaps a determining feature of the Gothic and certainly a theme of *The Castle of Otranto*, where the dynastic anxieties of Manfred become real terrors. However, 'The Nightmare' and *The Castle of Otranto* could be said to inspire two halves of *The Time Warrior*. If *Otranto* has author and reader travel backwards into an imaginary past kept at a safe distance, 'The Nightmare' has a figure from historical mythology – a demon from a superstitious age the audience thinks it has grown past – enter the present and claim someone on its own terms, much as Linx does. Fuseli's execution of 'The Nightmare' has been compared with the 'modernity' of the new wave of history paintings characterised by Benjamin West's 'The Death of Wolfe' (1770)[67]. West's decision to display General James Wolfe and his colleagues in dress authentic for their time – the battle

---

[65] Radcliffe, Michael, 'Fuseli: The Dramatic Moment', *The Times*, 18 January 1973; Bainbridge, Timothy, 'Romantic Artists', *The Spectator*, 24 March 1973.

[66] Tisdall, Caroline, 'Watercolour Mellon', *The Guardian* (26 February 1973).

[67] Powell, *Fuseli: The Nightmare*, p78.

of Quebec, 13 September 1759 – and not in classical garb shocked audiences with its immediacy. A comparison might be made with the way that, as a television-watching child in the 1970s, I found the shift between 'exterior' film and 'interior' studio videotape conveyed a move from the safely **outside** to the immediate domestic confinement of **indoors**, with fewer routes of escape. Likewise the arrival of the horrific amidst the everyday setting is more threatening than an entirely mythological scene.

Crises of Identity: *Frankenstein*

The evolution of the Gothic in the 19th century was shaped by competing desires for, and fears of, revolution, often in the same works. A generation formed by the French Revolution and succeeding French and Napoleonic wars lacked the confident condescension of a Horace Walpole. For Mary Shelley's *Frankenstein* (1818), Victor Frankenstein's obsession with past knowledge, in the form of superseded scientific theories, is not a stony path to redemption as it is for the present and former ruling families of Otranto, but a journey to oblivion which misunderstands creation as an emotionless act. Linx is a descendant of Frankenstein, whose methods had been embellished in transmission from book to stage to cinema.

Like successive Frankensteins, Linx works in secret from the world in a private laboratory. His dungeon-like arrangement contrasts with the 'solitary chamber, or rather cell, at the top of the house' used by Frankenstein in Mary Shelley's novel, or the lightning-attracting garrets of the first two Universal films of the 1930s, or the loft of Victor Frankenstein in Hammer's *The Curse of Frankenstein* (1957). Its grimy dankness makes the cellar perhaps even more literally a 'workshop of filthy creation'[68] than the upstairs charnel-house of *Frankenstein* the book. The nearest Linx has to the dead bodies used by Frankenstein are his enslaved human workforce; both are treated as commodities, with neither Linx nor Frankenstein showing compassion for their fellow beings. By making the abducted scientists toil unconsciously underground, Linx ensures that his workforce endure what is presented as a living death – the script for episode 1 describes them as going 'about their work with zombie-like concentration' while those for episodes 2 and 3 call them 'zombie scientists' or simply 'zombies' (a description that Dicks did not carry through to the novelisation) – while the being Frankenstein assembles from dead human tissue finds that human society has no place for the unwillingly resurrected. Both Linx and Frankenstein think they have mastered their natural environments, but neither has the means to escape from the legacy of their actions, though Linx's fate is more prosaic than Frankenstein's.

Frankenstein was set in a pre-revolutionary 18th century and posed as being rooted in earlier natural philosophy. However, its questions about reciprocal duties between individuals and its presentation of man and monster as divided selves were political and literary concerns alive in a Europe where all participating states had left the Revolutionary and Napoleonic Wars transformed constitutionally and territorially. The character of the victory settlement dissatisfied many elements of the coalition which had brought about Napoleon's fall. Domestically **Doctor Who** was itself a fiction addressed to a post-Second World War audience, comparable to, though much broader than, Mary Shelley's initial post-Napoleonic *Frankenstein* readership.

---

[68] Shelley, Mary, *Frankenstein, or the Modern Prometheus: the 1818 Text*, ed Nick Groom, p35.

At its inception in 1963, **Doctor Who** had been intended to make 'science' and 'history' accessible to a family viewership. Arguably 'science' represented Britain's journey into the 'white heat of technology'[69]; 'history' what it was building on. In posing with copies of *New Scientist* in the office for a *Radio Times* feature in 1970, Barry Letts and Terrance Dicks drew attention to one side of that legacy; the other was underplayed but present in the content of the first Pertwee year's serials, especially *Doctor Who and the Silurians* and *Inferno*[70].

The UK of the 1970s was itself in a Gothic crisis of multiple identities and yearnings for mislaid truths. A consensual view of society which had developed as a way of surviving the Second World War and its aftermath was challenged by views which denied its objectivity, with varying degrees of self-consciousness. These alternative outlooks could seem like returns to the prison of the subjective worldview, or as liberation of the imagination in the Gothic tradition. That liberation was accompanied by fear that Britain was a country at war with itself. While its leaders sought to present Britain as a modern, forward-looking European state, the country struggled to divest itself of colonial possessions around the world with minimal loss of money, access to their resources, and international standing. Meanwhile, it faced increasing antagonism within industry and lack of confidence in and within political leadership. Division manifested chiefly in the form of violence in Northern Ireland, but also through other challenges to the received political and social orders, including demands for autonomy in Scotland and Wales and the women's

---

[69] Misquoting a speech by Harold Wilson, leader of the Labour Party, on 1 October 1963.
[70] *Radio Times*, 9–15 May 1970.

liberation movement of which the production office of **Doctor Who** were particularly conscious when devising Sarah Jane Smith. It is not surprising that the satirical intent of the original storyline of *The Time Warrior* was assimilated within Gothic themes and trappings.

Legacies of the Robin Hoods

The Gothic of *The Time Warrior* involves science and its misapplication and the unveiling of the monstrous, but neither the philosophical exchanges of Mary Shelley nor the material horror of moral transgressions as realised in cinema adaptations would have been suitable for **Doctor Who** by themselves, nor would they have conveyed the atmosphere or setting required. The Gothic needed to be couched in a received depiction of the medieval past which owed more to 20th-century escapism.

Both Robert Holmes and Terrance Dicks would have expected a degree of audience familiarity with a cultural view of the Middle Ages shared by film and television and derived from earlier popular fiction. This has long been recognised by **Doctor Who** commentators. In a 1981 article in DWM, **Doctor Who**'s early historical stories were contextualised as the BBC's response to a broadcasting environment in the early 1960s where filmed adventure series set in a heroic past were among the major attractions of the BBC's advertising-funded competitors, the ITV companies[71]. The argument made by its author

---

[71]   'For the years prior to **Doctor Who** the commercial television channels had been raking in large audiences of children with series such as **Robin Hood** [...] King John [...] was as wicked as ever he was while the Lionheart-supporting outlaw was whiter than white [...] The simple fact of the matter was that such formula-written productions gained good viewing

that the historical stories of **Doctor Who** closely followed ITV models is open to question, but it is difficult to disagree that the ITV 'swashbucklers' established precedents with which **Doctor Who** was bound to be compared. The series **The Adventures of Robin Hood** (1955-59) had led the way in determining the form of the television 'swashbuckler'. It was produced by Sapphire Films, an independent production company, and funded through distributors who aimed to make back their investment through sales. This model was usual for television series made on film in the 1950s and 1960s.

Robin Hood was one of several series made for television with an international – principally American – audience in mind, but was the first to make a success of a British historical adventure setting. The first episode of **Robin Hood**, written by the blacklisted Hollywood screenwriter Ring Lardner Jr, combines the derring-do of swordplay amidst the aristocratic theme of dispossession of knightly lands and the more populist one of a cruel regime which punishes the starving. With these comes an element of light contemporary satire, as Robin of Locksley returns from war to find a changed society which doesn't know what to do with demobbed crusaders and at worst (in the eyes of the Sheriff of Nottingham's clerk) regards them as expecting privileged treatment based on a false sense of entitlement. Although the parallel isn't exact, as the crusaders are specifically identified as volunteers rather than conscripts, the clerk's remark would have resonated with former service personnel in the worldwide audience, probably watching with their children[72]. The contemporaneity is too

---

numbers and the **Doctor Who** producers were keen to capture these for their history-related shows.'
(Bentham, Jeremy, 'Living in the Past', DWM #56, September 1981.)
[72] **The Adventures of Robin Hood**: *The Coming of Robin Hood.*

masked to be truly 'agitational' in the sense later meant by **Doctor Who**'s initial guiding spirit Sydney Newman[73], but anticipates the paralleling enjoyed by *The Time Warrior* and helps the programme's sense of immediacy.

Later episodes provided more precedents for *The Time Warrior*. The episode *The May Queen* includes the line 'England is sick. With the king away the barons vie for power. They steal the land of better men who are at the wars.'[74] While their depictions of competing barons are different, both **Robin Hood** and *The Time Warrior* use 'the wars' as a convenient distancing from the issues surrounding the Crusades. 'The wars' also can also generalise the time period to a non-specific 'the Middle Ages'. The broadcast *Time Warrior* never specifies a period, but it also lacks **Robin Hood**'s generally optimistic portrayal of the trend towards social justice. The poor of *The Time Warrior* are either fatalistically oppressed (the kitchen women at Irongron's castle), happy with their lot as servants (Hal the archer and his 'girlfriend' Mary, although Mary's dialogue disappeared by the time of broadcast) or banded together under Irongron to perform deeds of cruelty associated in the **Robin Hood** tradition with the 'Norman' aristocracy. The nobility of *The Time Warrior* is ineffectual (Edward of Wessex) or devious (Lady Eleanor) but jealous of their status. There is no equivalent to *The May Queen*'s Walter Donnington, happy to be seen covered in hay despite his mother's argument that his dignity is sullied, or Robin himself, except perhaps the Doctor; but

---

[73] Sendall, Bernard *Origin and Foundation, 1946-62*, 1982, vol 1 of *Independent Television in Britain* (1982-90), p338.

[74] Cited in Chapman, James, 'The Adventures of Robin Hood and the Origins of the Television Swashbuckler', *Media History* 17:3, 2011, p279.

he is a complex creation representing several strands of identity.

Another episode which plays on contemporary themes close to those of *The Time Warrior* is *The Genius* (first broadcast by ATV London on 13 April 1958) where a mathematical genius is smuggled out of the grasp of an emissary of Prince John who wants to use his calculations to build more advanced weaponry. The relative levels of civilisation (Linx's homeworld and Earth, medieval England and modern Britain, Sontaran and Gallifreyan ethical systems) and concerns about what use human beings would put advanced technology, are all preoccupations of *The Time Warrior*.

Just as, if not more, important to *The Time Warrior* were earlier cinema versions of Robin Hood. The outfits worn by Hal the Archer – a figure whose archery skills rival those of Robin Hood – and Sarah Jane Smith in her 'men's clothes' echo those worn in the Warner Bros film *The Adventures of Robin Hood* (1938), albeit dyed in dirtier hues than those which suited three-strip Technicolor and which clad Errol Flynn, Olivia de Havilland, and their fellow cast members. There are a few echoes of Erich Wolfgang Korngold's score for the 1938 film in Dudley Simpson's music for *The Time Warrior*; not in the jaunty main theme, but the drumbeats which introduce it and which occasionally act as a countermelody, and in the use of horns. However, it is the differences which are more marked: Simpson's atonal dissonance is almost entirely distinct from Korngold's expansive late Romanticism, although there is also an echo of the pounding countermelody from the theme music of the 1950s television series. Robin Hood is important to *The Time Warrior* even though there is no single Robin Hood analogue in the story. Aspects of his character are divided between the Doctor, Sarah, Irongron and Hal. However, the spread of Robin Hood in popular culture means that *The Time Warrior* is inevitably borrowing from aspects of versions of the legend or in dialogue with them.

With the 1950s television series having faded from regular repeat runs by the ITV companies[75], 1938's *The Adventures of Robin Hood* was by 1973 arguably more current than its namesake, the Richard Greene series. A newspaper preview of a television screening hailed the film as 'a classic, beautifully staged Hollywood adventure yarn that remains as fresh and Lincoln green as ever'[76]. In this case, *The Adventures of Robin Hood* was being shown by BBC One on Friday 9 July 1971 at 7:20pm, the main event of BBC One's evening. This was the film's second showing on BBC One, the first having been on Saturday 20 December 1969 at 6:45pm, just over a month after the start of colour transmissions of BBC One and two weeks to the day before Jon Pertwee's first episode of **Doctor Who** was broadcast[77]. The 1971 screening was itself an hour after the start time of the repeat of episode 4 of Pertwee's first story, Robert Holmes' *Spearhead from Space*[78]. It is tempting to make correlations, but authors do not necessarily watch repeats of their earlier work and then gain inspiration from the programme scheduled next but one after it.

The most direct reference to a screen Robin Hood in the script for *The Time Warrior*, however, is to an earlier version still than that of 1938. In the rehearsal script for episode 4, the Doctor, disguised as a

---

[75] By 1971 only HTV Cymru Wales was showing the series, according to *The Guardian* listings, last broadcasting it on 21 February 1972.
[76] *The Observer*, 4 July 1971.
[77] 'High Adventure: The Adventures of Robin Hood', *BBC Genome*.
[78] 'The Movie Crazy Years: The Adventures of Robin Hood', *BBC Genome*.

'robot knight', presents himself as a gift from Linx to Irongron as in the broadcast version. The fight sequence which follows envisaged much more physical action for the armoured Jon Pertwee than could be realised:

> THE MEN AT ARMS DRAW SWORDS AND JOIN IN [Irongron's and Bloodaxe's joint assault on the Doctor]. THERE NOW ENSUES A SPECTACULAR FIGHT IN WHICH THE DOCTOR IN AN AMAZING DISPLAY OF SWORDSMANSHIP HAS TO DEFEND HIMSELF AGAINST HIS NUMEROUS OPPONENTS. THIS HE DOES, WITH MUCH DOUGLAS FAIRBANKS-TYPE LEAPING ON TABLES AND HURLING OF FURNITURE. THIS SEQUENCE SHOULD BE AS LONG EXCITING AND SPECTACULAR AS POSSIBLE.

'As long exciting and spectacular as possible' proved to be 'not at all', as in the camera script and as broadcast Irongron's men at arms never get as far as joining in. Once Irongron has resolved to 'try this creature's strength to the utmost', the transmitted episode rejoins Sarah in Irongron's kitchen. However, the script's appeal to the memory of Douglas Fairbanks didn't end there. Fairbanks had defined the historical action-hero in the Hollywood of the 1910s and 1920s in a series of performances of which *Douglas Fairbanks in Robin Hood* (1922) was the most lavish and most expensive, with huge sets, expansive use of locations, and crowds of extras in arrays of medieval fashions. Fairbanks wrote and produced as well as starred in the film. Fairbanks' Robert, Earl of Huntingdon, only becomes the bejerkined feathered-capped Robin Hood for the last hour of the film (which runs over two), but the staid crusader lord turns into an ebulliently dashing hero who can crawl down castle walls, jump from high windows, and leap across battlements while inept guards seek him below.

By 1973 action techniques pioneered by Fairbanks had been transmitted through copying, homage and pastiche. Richard Lester's *The Three Musketeers* (1973) was already anticipated (while *The Time Warrior* was being written) as a self-conscious blend of send-up and social realism. A few years later, cultural historian Jeffrey Richards ruled that the 1970s was 'an age in which parody flourishes in the absence of true creative spark' where 'the underlying ethic (of the swashbuckler) has been irreparably undermined.' Yet for *The Time Warrior*, its citation of Fairbanks was surely an appeal to authority and authenticity. **Doctor Who** was not addressed to the irony-seeking cinemagoer who knew that the medium was 'now feeding more than ever before on its mythic past'[79] and accepted the invitation to join the feeding frenzy, but to children and their parents who either did not know to be cynical, or who wanted to be brought out of their cynicism. Fairbanks' history in comedy and his athleticism made him an obvious precedent for the comedian and sometime motorcycle stunt rider Jon Pertwee. Pertwee's physicality was by *The Time Warrior* established as a signature of his performance as the Doctor, even if in many scenes (as acknowledged at several points in the camera script) the Doctor's stunts were undertaken by Terry Walsh.

Ivanhoe and Identity

The 20th-century adaptations of Robin Hood discussed above drew on the Gothic romanticism of an imagined medieval England largely established by Sir Walter Scott's *Ivanhoe*, first published in 1820. Where the antecedents of *The Time Warrior* are concerned, *Ivanhoe*

---

[79] Richards, Jeffrey, *Swordsmen of the Screen*, p24.

was a vital point of transition between the Gothic and the Romantic. The Romantic movement was less concerned with finding dissonance between past and present and within human perceptions of the world, but in reconciling the present with the past and finding beauty and principle there rather than degradation.

Ivanhoe bore much of the responsibility for Victorian obsession with medievalism. Like Horace Walpole before him, Scott wrote his preface in a fictitious guise, posing to be a new writer at odds with the dry antiquarianism of existing treatments of the Middle Ages, and pretending to be adapting a newly-discovered manuscript. The hero of the novel, a Saxon noble called Wilfred of Ivanhoe, is governed by a strictly observed code of chivalry. *Ivanhoe* presents late 12th-century England as a polarised and cruel society, divided between Norman conquerors and Saxon conquered, but also between a bi-ethnic ruling class and their enslaved thralls. Violence from the ruling elite, principally made up of Normans, is commonplace, aggravated by the absence of Richard I from his kingdom following the Third Crusade. An outsider, the Templar knight Sir Brian de Bois-Guilbert, watches the struggle between Saxon and Norman but participates only to pursue his own agenda, believing his rationalism makes him superior to social conventions. His beliefs derive in part from his contact with the Islamic world, from which he has also brought his silent Saracen servants. Meanwhile, a Jewish merchant, Isaac of York, and his daughter Rebecca are treated as feared strangers by other characters despite the gentiles' reliance on them for medical and technical assistance as well as the despised financial aid.

This is a selective summary which flags up story elements with parallels in *The Time Warrior*. The simplistic and inaccurate depiction of medieval England as divided between Saxon and Norman 'came to dominate 19th-century views' of Robin Hood, and associated the character with a particular racial politics of freedom-loving English genius which inevitably led to the domination of the British Empire over the rest of the world[80]. In the mid-20th century cinema inspired by *Ivanhoe*, and not only the 1952 Metro-Goldwyn-Mayer adaptation of Scott's book, the blending of Saxon and Norman is perhaps open to reading as a post-war allegory of reconciliation between former enemies in the face of a greater threat[81].

Despite its unapologetically blatant level of invention, Scott's *Ivanhoe* became an inspiration for English people looking to conserve their sense of identity following the upheaval of the Napoleonic Wars, while threatened by anti-industrialisation protesters the Luddites and political reformers on one hand, and a militarised state on the other. One of the ways in which its indirect legacy is felt in *The Time Warrior* is through Sarah's assumption on her first arrival in the Middle Ages that she is at a medieval pageant[82]. The popularity of *Ivanhoe* encouraged the growth of the historical pageant, a day when participants would dress in historic costume or approximations of it. The most famous example was the Eglinton Tournament of 28 to 30 August 1839, where Archibald William Montgomerie, 13th Earl of Eglinton, a Scottish peer with a surname of Norman origin, hosted a series of jousts and melées at his castle

---

[80] Barczewski, Stephanie L, *Myth and National Identity in Nineteenth-Century*, pp129ff.

[81] This and other Cold War parallels in 1950s adventure films are discussed in Richards, *Swordsmen of the Screen*, Chapter 4.

[82] 'Oh, it must be some sort of pageant,' remarks Sarah outside the castle in Part One, before she is dragged into it.

of Eglinton in Ayrshire. These were not mock battles but wholehearted attempts to revive medieval knightly combat as the proper recreation for the aristocracy. Participants were largely aristocrats with Tory party backgrounds whose families had governed for most of the Revolutionary and Napoleonic period, but had been displaced from power in the 1830s. They trained for a year beforehand and where they had no suits of armour in their own collections, hired them from such sources as the Tower of London or commissioned their own. Lavish heraldic shields, banners and gowns were also part of the spectacle. A banquet and ball in more modern setting accompanied the events. The event was derided for the frequent interruptions of heavy rain and for the crippling expense suffered by Eglinton himself, but it was a huge spectator event, with 100,000 people attending.

The tournament established Eglinton's political career as a champion of tradition in British national life and as a defender of Scottish national culture, but also encouraged imitators on a variety of scales[83]. The heart of British identity, or of its component identities, was located in the past rather than the present. At a later civic event, the Colchester Pageant of 1909, 3,000 performers took part in a sequence of events including Boadicea's defeat of the Romans around 60 CE, the rise of oyster fisheries on the Essex coast, and the siege of Colchester in 1648. Political and aristocratic history and the social life of the common people were blended into one through

[83] Pentland, Gordon, 'The Eglinton Tournament 1839: A Victorian Take on the Anglo-Scottish Rivalry', *History of Parliament*, 4 September 2014.

mass performance[84]. Communities continued to organise such events throughout the 1960s and into the 1970s.

After discounting that she is at a local pageant, Sarah moves on to rationalise her surroundings as a fully restored medieval castle with professional re-enactors playing historical characters. Re-enactment, a more specialised form of historical recreation than the pageant, gained ground during the 20th century both as pastime for volunteers and as a commercial enterprise. The development of the stately home as tourist attraction by aristocratic families needing new sources of revenue led to the inclusion of medieval-themed events if the venue was appropriate. An obvious example was Warwick Castle, promoted as the best-preserved medieval castle in England, whose owner Lord Brooke mounted re-enactments of the siege of the castle during the English Civil War, staged a 'medieval fair' in 1971, and sold places at medieval banquets[85].

Early 1970s Medievalism in Film and Television

Dramatic conventions prevent Sarah from making the leap to realising that she, Irongron, Bloodaxe and the rest of the 'scurvy, smelly lot'[86] are all characters in a television programme. If she had done, it might not have surprised her. Commissioning a **Doctor Who**

---

[84] Thompson, Kathryn, 'Godebog!', *The Redress of the Past: Historical Pageants in Britain*, 18 April 2016.

[85] *The Times,* 29 May and 26 June 1971. Brooke's father, Fulke Greville, seventh Earl of Warwick of the Greville family, had transferred the house to his son to avoid death duties; as a film actor in 1930s Hollywood (Michael Brooke) he had appeared in *The Dawn Patrol* with Errol Flynn.

[86] Part Two script. The line is cut off after 'scurvy' in performance as David Daker as Irongron interrupts Elisabeth Sladen.

story set in the Middle Ages was in keeping with the medievalist turn in contemporary media. It's likely that the production team would have known that Disney intended to release their animated feature *Robin Hood* during 1973. For an older audience, 1973 saw the release of the movie *Gawain and the Green Knight*, based on the Middle English poem. This had been filmed at locations in Cheshire, suggested by textual evidence as the home county of the anonymous author, the 'Gawain Poet'. These included Peckforton Castle, which provided the exteriors for *The Time Warrior* in May 1973[87]. Peckforton was not a medieval castle at all, but a 19th-century creation of the architect Anthony Salvin (1799-1881). Salvin worked in a spirit which owed something to that of the Eglinton Tournament, in that rather than create a baroque tribute to an age safely past, as Walpole had done at Strawberry Hill, his medievalist architectural creations reflected a mid-19th century ideal that the authentic English spirit was to be found in earlier times.

The first choice had been Castell Coch in Glamorgan, a late 19th-century recreation (albeit with many historical inaccuracies and anachronisms) of a castle first built in the 12th and 13th centuries, but it was being conserved by the Department of the Environment. Production assistant Marcia Wheeler thought Peckforton, in private hands, had a 'slightly phony quality, machine-cut stone and so on, which in a way was perfect for **Doctor Who** – it had this slight unreality which was in a way just right'[88].

One might disagree with Wheeler on the aesthetic of **Doctor Who** in general, but she recognised the kinship between the 19th-century

---

[87] A location photograph appeared in *The Guardian*, 22 February 1972.
[88] *Toby Hadoke's Whosround* #84.

architecture and *The Time Warrior*'s medievalism. She seems to have been unaware that although a Victorian creation, Peckforton Castle was built with defence in mind. It was commissioned by John Jervis Tollemache (1805-90), then the largest landowner in Cheshire. Born John Jervis Halliday, he and his father had assumed the Tollemache surname in 1821 on inheriting a portion of the estates of the Tollemache family through his grandmother. Tollemache's life was driven by the need to consolidate his inheritance and his status in the upper gentry; a career as an MP and a series of offices held culminated in his elevation to the House of Lords in 1876 as Baron Tollemache. Peckforton was built on one of the estates he acquired by purchase rather than inheritance, and its walls and fortifications were strong enough to protect himself and his family from an imagined assault by the factory workers of Lancashire (Manchester was only 30 miles away) and Cheshire should they arm themselves against the ruling landed class[89]. Tollemache demonstrated that he was no Sir Edward of Wessex feebly waiting for rescue, but despite his lineage as the grandson and great-grandson of earls, there was something of a legitimated Irongron about his determination to establish his power as a partly new-minted landowner by force of arms.

One contemporary television launch which might have encouraged the commissioning of *The Time Warrior* was **Arthur of the Britons** (1972-73), whose first series began on ITV on Wednesday 6 December 1972 at 4:50pm, an established children's drama slot[90]. **Arthur of the Britons** was a product both of the commercial attraction borne by the internationally-known Arthurian legends,

---

[89] Jill Allibone, *Anthony Salvin*, pp98-106.
[90] *The Times,* 6 December 1972.

and of regulatory concerns in that the series represented the character of Wales and the West of England, the 'dual region' covered by the ITV contractor who produced it, HTV. Additional factors were the wish to present a break with the romanticised past of the ITV swashbucklers and present a 'realistic' Arthur eking an existence on the frontier between Saxon and Celt in post-Roman Britain. There were no castles in this version, unlike in Sapphire Films' follow-up to **The Adventures of Robin Hood**, **The Adventures of Sir Lancelot** (1956-57). **Arthur of the Britons** had fleeting ties of personnel to **Doctor Who** in that its initial devisers and lead writers were Bob Baker and Dave Martin, contributors to **Doctor Who** since the 1971 season, although in the event they were eased out early in production[91]. The medievalism of *The Time Warrior*, with its dishevelled and brutal Irongron and Bloodaxe, owes something to the mood for deromanticisation represented by **Arthur of the Britons**, although it can be argued in the case of the latter that all it offers is an alternative romance of a post-civilisation society not that far removed, perhaps, from the post-industrial world envisaged by the Wholeweal Community of the **Doctor Who** story preceding *The Time Warrior, The Green Death* (1973).

Other strands of medievalism in early 1970s television included the first colour Sunday afternoon classic serial on BBC One. **Ivanhoe**, a 10-part adaptation of Scott's story by Alexander Baron, directed by **Doctor Who** regular David Maloney, began on 4 January 1970. Its colourful costumes owed much to 19th-century paintings, and writing and performance were very conscious of the unhistorical nature of Scott's depiction of the reign of Richard I; this was storybook rather than historical drama. By 1973, the younger part of

---

[91] Baker, Bob, *K-9 Stole My Trousers*, pp103-06.

The Time Warrior's audience might have been most familiar with the world of knights and castles and crusades from **The Adventures of Sir Prancelot**, a series of 31 five-minute episodes shown every weekday afternoon on BBC One from Thursday 13 January 1972. These were commissioned for the 5:44pm slot before the main evening news, established by **The Magic Roundabout** as a place for animations aimed at a pre-school audience but which could be appreciated by adults. Described as 'the adventures of an inventive knight on his journey to the crusades', **Sir Prancelot** was written and illustrated by John Ryan and narrated by Peter Hawkins. It began a repeat run on Wednesday 12 July 1972, ending on 25 August, and a third on Monday 5 March 1973, while *The Time Warrior* was being written. Sir Prancelot was a jovial, white-haired knight and eccentric inventor who eventually returned to England from the Holy Land by home-made rocket ship. To a young child he was not too far removed as a character from Jon Pertwee's Doctor.

The twice-weekly children's magazine programme **Blue Peter** (1958-) had a strong strand of historical items in the early 1970s. Most of these were features relating to history post-1500, including those relating to BBC programmes such as the items on the costumes of **The Six Wives of Henry VIII** (15 February 1971) and **War and Peace** (28 September 1972). The end of 1972 and early 1973 saw attention being paid to earlier periods including Roman sewers and walls and medieval subjects including a Viking house in York; Rahere, founder of St Bartholomew's Hospital in London; and St David [92].

Even if BBC children's programmes hadn't specifically addressed the

---

[92] 29 January, 1 February and 1 March 1973 respectively. Marson, Richard, *Blue Peter: Inside the Archives*, pp106, 116, 118, 120-1.

Middle Ages often in the early 1970s, other programmes children might have watched had done so. **Tomorrow's World** on 24 December 1971 was a Christmas special entitled *Tomorrow's World visits Yesterday's World*. This came from 'the historic splendour of Bunratty Castle' (in County Clare, Ireland, intriguingly outside the UK) and promised 'an extravaganza of anachronism' as presenters Raymond Baxter, James Burke and Michael Rodd tested a 1904 tram, dabbled in alchemy and found 'an unusual way of making Christmas trees'. They were joined by actors Hugh Griffith ('the baron who prefers the technology of yesterday') and Nerys Hughes ('the damsel of many parts') while television chef Clement Freud did some medieval cooking[93]. A year later **Holiday '73** featured 'Northumbria: A holiday kingdom of ancient history, castles and medieval junketing. But do you know where it is, how much it costs, how you get there?'[94] **Doctor Who** might have replied that more appropriate questions might have been when it was, that it might cost the fate of humanity, and that getting there by TARDIS was better than using osmic projection.

So After All That, When is The *Time Warrior* Set?

When writing his initial story proposal, Robert Holmes chose as its historical setting the reign of King John, from 1199 to 1216. Irongron was presented as a baron 'owing allegiance to a greater territorial leader, Kingjohn' and was therefore 'under hostile pressure from neighbouring groups of creatures'[95]. The historian's assumption might be that Holmes was misremembering the period when Richard

---

[93] **Tomorrow's World**, BBC One London, 24 December 1971.
[94] **Holiday '73**, BBC One London, 28 December 1972.
[95] Molesworth, *Robert Holmes*, p205

I was on crusade and assumed that John actually usurped the throne during that time. The authors of *The Discontinuity Guide* located the story in Richard's reign, perhaps influenced by the novelisation where Sir Edward was 'still wasted by the fever he had brought back from the Holy Land'[96]. Alternatively, Holmes might have been inspired by the latter part of John's reign, when, in 1212, after several years of consolidating his hold on England and his overlordship in Scotland, Wales, and Ireland, a series of misjudged aggressive actions in Wales and successful resistance by the Welsh revealed how thin John's support among the great landholders in England actually was and several barons rose in rebellion.

Presenting Irongron as a rebellious thief of peasant stock is unhistorical, in that the 'robber barons' of the era, in both history and fiction, were noblemen of knightly background, such as John's own favourite Falkes de Bréauté[97], but Irongron is the sort of disreputable figure Holmes enjoyed writing. Holmes', and the audience's, vague awareness of periods of political disorder is used to promote this would-be baron from the criminal class, and the 'bad king' of the Middle Ages with highest name recognition is probably John.

In his domestic policy and his continental forays, John was aided by his half-brother, William Longespée, Earl of Salisbury (c1167-1226). Longespée's prominence as an ally of John might lie behind the

---

[96] Cornell, Paul, Martin Day and Keith Topping, *Doctor Who: The Discontinuity Guide*, p157; Dicks, *The Time Warrior*, p37.

[97] Power, D.J., 'Bréauté, Sir Falkes de', *Oxford Dictionary of National Biography*. A 1903 novel, *The Robber Baron of Bedford Castle*, by AJ Foster and EE Cuthell, depicted the Bréautés as a clan of cowardly and brutal villains, albeit more aristocratic than Irongron.

mentions of 'my lord Salisbury' as Sir Edward's ally in *The Time Warrior*. While it seems unlikely that Robert Holmes did any extensive historical research, given the short period which he had to write *The Time Warrior*, and his own aversion to didactic content in **Doctor Who**, Longespée is prominently mentioned in one of the first ports of call for the researcher on the period, the article on King John in the *Dictionary of National Biography*[98]. However, in Holmes' initial thinking Irongron, not Sir Edward, was the ally of John; though it's conceivable a harangued castle-owner seeking a quiet life would try to negotiate with the superior of an unruly neighbour.

One problem with a date in the reign of John is the name of one of the principal characters. The name Edward was not used by the landed and knightly class in England in John's reign, although like some other names of Anglo-Saxon and Danish origin it persisted (though was not common) among the peasantry[99]. The Norman and Angevin kings of England traced their legitimacy in part to the nomination of William of Normandy as his successor by Edward the Confessor, last king of England of the old family of the kings of Wessex, while John's father, Henry II, secured the recognition by Pope Alexander III of Edward the Confessor as a saint in 1161. John's son Henry III made the veneration of Edward's tomb at Westminster Abbey a central part of his kingship and named his two sons Edward and Edmund, after the Confessor and another Anglo-Saxon royal saint, and only then did the name Edward began to be adopted by the English aristocracy. Allowing that the nearest to a firm date for

---

[98] Hunt, W, 'John (1167?-1216), King of England' in Sidney Lee, ed, *Dictionary of National Biography* vol 29 (1892), pp402-17.
[99] Postles, Dave, *Naming the People of England, c.1100-1350*, p15, 18, 29, 53.

the story is in a later **Doctor Who** serial, *The Sontaran Experiment*, where Sarah declares that 'Linx [was] destroyed in the 13th century'[100], then perhaps *The Time Warrior* takes place during the reign of Edward I, a king frequently away fighting, whether on crusade or in Wales, Scotland and France. There was no Earl of Salisbury at this time, but then there was no Irongron either[101]. This theory would be more vulnerable had a line in the rehearsal script for episode 2 remained: where on broadcast the Doctor told Professor Rubeish, 'You've been brought back to the early years of the Middle Ages,' the rehearsal script gave a more definite 'early years of the 13th century,' bringing John's reign back into focus.

The Time Warrior's creative appropriation of earlier medievalism indicates that a narrow dating of the story misses the point. Sir Edward lives at Wessex Castle, an anachronistically named stronghold, as the name Wessex for one of the constituent parts of England fell out of use following the Norman Conquest of 1066. It's probably the uses of 'Wessex' and of 'Edward' which led Jean-Marc Lofficier originally to date the story to about the year 800[102]. However, the Anglo-Saxon names point less to a time than to a tradition, the legacy of *Ivanhoe*. Irongron dismisses writing as 'Norman scribbles' (episode 1) and the voice the Doctor adopts when about to divest himself of the robot knight's armour as that of a 'Norman ninny' (episode 4). These are codes from *Ivanhoe* and

---

[100] *The Sontaran Experiment*, Part Two.
[101] This dating is shared by two **Doctor Who** chronologies: Parkin, Lance, and Lars Pearson, *Ahistory*, 4th edition, chooses 'c.1273' (p1107) and Preddle, Jon, *Timelink*, 2nd edition, '1274' (p234).
[102] Jean-Marc Lofficier, *The Doctor Who Programme Guide Volume 2*, p34. Lofficier later amended his dating to 'c.1190'. Lofficier, *Doctor Who – The Terrestrial Index*, p37.

20th-century interpretations of Robin Hood rather than an explicit determination to identify the ruling class of the story as Norman. They mark Irongron as non-elite but also as uncouth and unpolished, at odds with *Ivanhoe*'s courteous Saxon nobles but somewhat in keeping with its illiterate thralls Gurth and Wamba.

Meanwhile Sir Edward, as well as displaying the sickliness which tradition associates with Edward the Confessor, has some similarities to two prominent Saxon noblemen invented by Scott, Cedric of Rotherwood and Athelstane of Coningsburgh. He is 'fairly young', according to the camera script, but is ineffectual and lacks the will to put his plans into action, much like Athelstane. Both Edward and Athelstane have agendas set for them by others, Lady Eleanor in Edward's case and Cedric in Athelstane's. Where, in the event, Athelstane acknowledges Richard I as the true inheritor of the Saxon crown of England, once the Doctor has helped despatch Linx and Irongron, Edward's lack of authority can only rely on the support of his wife and Hal the archer, and the expected return of his neighbours of similar rank and outlook from the wars. The time of *The Time Warrior* is slyly achronological, perhaps less heavy-handed than its 21st-century successor *Robot of Sherwood* (2014), but placed at the overlap between documentary history, the Middle Ages of popular culture, and skeins of Gothic and Romantic motifs.

Symbolism and Relationships

Where *Ivanhoe* and its 19th-century imitators concerned themselves with the endurance of a liberty-loving and martial English spirit, *The Time Warrior* employs their symbolism with little faith in these sometime virtues. The liberties and martial skills in ascendancy for most of the story are those of Irongron — illiterate, aggressive disparager of Normans, and protégé of the intergalactic imperialist Linx. A Gothic dissociation appears in the displacement of chivalry from the setting in which the audience expects to find it, replaced by ineffectual nobility, assassination plots, and a monster in the cellar. *The Time Warrior*'s medievalism could not exist without the Gothicism of Walpole and Fuseli, nor the Romanticism of Scott and Eglinton. However, its interpretations are contemporary to 1973 and are not transplanted awkwardly from earlier periods. Robert Holmes tells his story through a series of contrasts, not only between an imagined medieval and an equally imagined modern, but between different projections of the Middle Ages in which their potential for the uncanny is balanced with the familiar – Holmes' characters, like Walpole's, responding as close as possible to real people. The script by turns flatters and baits the sceptical viewer while plunging everyone into an adventure story which depends for its 'realism' on the conflict between pairings of attitudes presented as progressive and regressive. This it does by using a series of doubled characters, not always themselves clearly medieval and modern in origin but keeping those labels in mind. While the central pairing is that of the Doctor and Sarah Jane Smith, they only form a bond through a series of other alliances and antagonisms. The principal antagonism, and the one around which the other relationships orbit, is that of the Doctor and Linx.

CHAPTER 3: 'THAT IS HOW HE WOULD APPEAR IN HUMAN EYES'

Space and Time for the Doctor and Linx

A mysterious object trails across the sky, startling the local authorities. A capsule from space appears from nowhere in the forest, containing an alien being who needs help from paramilitaries to repair his craft. The off-worlder is charismatic with an engaging if misleading air of taking his earthly companions into his confidence. His technology is of a familiar form, but is inexplicable to his hosts, who hope for their own reasons that the visitor will remain for a long time.

The above paragraph offers a brief description of a character who could be either the Doctor or Linx. The parallels are obvious, especially with *Spearhead from Space*; but so are the objections. While Irongron and his men saw Linx's vessel cross the sky and fall to Earth, the UNIT officer and her technician saw Nestene energy units, not the TARDIS. The UNIT personnel identified an enemy, while it's Irongron who finds an ally. However, this latter statement is open to challenge, and it's part of the Doctor's function in this story to point out why.

The Two Heroes

Dramatically, the Doctor and Linx are designed to shadow each other throughout the serial. The audience's bias towards the Doctor is challenged by devices which encourage complicity with Linx. At the outset of Linx's relationship with the viewer, the Sontaran is probably more attractive than the figures with whom he is being contrasted, Irongron and his men. Irongron, Bloodaxe and company are dirty, in old clothes, frustrated by the fare at the castle not matching their ideals. In a sense they are boys who have found that the toy they had longed for and finally won doesn't deliver the enjoyment they had hoped. Linx is a shining, almost godlike figure, rather like the knights in Chrétien de Troyes' *Perceval* (written in the 1180s) encountered in the forest by the young hero[103]. As befits him at the start of a serial, he's an emblem of possibility, both for Irongron and for the viewer. Unlike Irongron, he is fluent in the technobabble of **Doctor Who**, a challenge to proprietorship of the series. The experienced viewer of the series, as well as the inhabitant of a gadget-reliant 1970s household, would share Linx's sense of superiority to Irongron. Linx also comes very close indeed to addressing the audience directly. When resolving to take the technology 'from those who have [it]', he makes a turn away from Irongron of about 110 degrees, very narrowly avoiding speaking into the camera. Linx seems to anticipate the addresses to the camera of a later Robert Holmes creation, Morgus in *The Caves of Androzani*.

The challenge Linx lays down to the Doctor is to defend his position as the title character. The series had not always forced the Doctor into this position. For most if not all of the first Doctor's era he was intimately linked to the enigma which drove the series on, almost a personification of the inability of the TARDIS to guide itself. The second Doctor continued this, with an added accentuation of the moral compunction to interfere in events developed under the first. With the third Doctor matters were complicated by the character's exile to Earth. This Doctor could not leave the consequences of his actions behind him, but the format of a series of serials allowed

---

[103] Lupack, Alan, *The Oxford Guide to Arthurian Literature and Legend*, p214.

limited range for the realisation of the impact of those consequences. In season seven this problem was accommodated in the frosty and combative relationship between the Doctor and the Brigadier. Season eight thaws this through giving the third Doctor a larger company to play with, drawing on the lead actor's background in radio comedy with its ensemble casts.

The manipulation of star personas by the production process is an old theme in **Doctor Who** criticism, but its role in storytelling is undeniable. Anecdotally, the popularity of the Master was regarded by Jon Pertwee as a threat to his own status. While Delgado might have challenged Pertwee's charisma, his character rarely challenged the Doctor's heroism. The arrival of the Master and of Jo Grant allowed a renewed emphasis on heroic traits in the Doctor. The Doctor's heroism is presented from season eight as that of an educator, a discoverer and a protector. All three qualities are intellectual, but the third is also physical. The intellectual qualities are presented in a moral framework: for example, dialogue and performance establish that it is irresponsible, incurious, needlessly destructive and (both consequently and independently) wrong for the British Ministry of Defence (with the collaboration of a captive UNIT) to shoot down the enigmatic 'comet' (subsequently revealed to be the parasitic entity Axos) in episode 1 of *The Claws of Axos* (1971). The Doctor succinctly extracts these points from the scene with the line 'Shoot first and think afterwards, is that it?' and when Axos simply disappears to avoid the missile strike, it is the Doctor who gains authority and snaps civil servant Chinn out of his paralysis so the missiles can be aborted. While it's the Doctor's role as mentor to the underqualified but intuitively intelligent Jo Grant which is best remembered, in *Axos* the Doctor becomes tutor to representatives of the British scientific establishment, pointedly not taking leadership of official research into Axonite and instead using an advisory role to encourage scientist Winser to question his cultural assumptions and his methodology, with limited success.

Much of this is repeated, even burlesqued, in *The Time Warrior*. The Doctor berates the military on contemporary Earth for asking the wrong questions and using the wrong methods. His advanced learning and skills as a technologist open the possibilities to solving the problem of the missing scientists. In the Middle Ages he becomes the educator of the enfeebled knight Sir Edward and his more assertive spouse Lady Eleanor, teaching them to think their way round a problem which, culturally, they see purely in terms of force of arms. By *The Time Warrior* it's established that the Doctor has skills in physical combat, but they are never exercised for their own sake. Indeed, in episode 2 of *The Green Death* the Doctor apologises to the Global Chemicals security guards he hurts, though Pertwee's delivery suggests the Doctor is not especially concerned. In *The Time Warrior*, there are convenient thugs in Irongron's service to overcome for whom no remorse is shown. Nevertheless, Irongron and his band are presented as a force for greed, ignorance and violence, opposed to the Doctor's talent for identifying higher purposes and promoting them consensually.

These, by *The Time Warrior*, have become the liberal humanism of a privileged time and space traveller. In *The Claws of Axos* the Doctor could not necessarily be trusted to practise what he preached. In episode 2 he experiments with Axonite in the hope of repairing the TARDIS, an incident which lends credibility to his apparently self-interested collaboration with the Master in episode 4. This turns out to be a feint for the trapping of Axos in a time loop, though the

Doctor did hope to escape and then resume his travels in time and space rather than return to his exile on Earth. By *The Time Warrior* the Doctor's exile has ended and he is free to intervene from a disinterested position. His most heroic act is possibly his attempt to persuade Linx to renounce his course of action and collaborate in the compassionate return of the scientists, who he regards as fellow sentient beings worthy of respect. For this, the Doctor is blasted down at the conclusion of episode 3. Even after this, the Doctor's hand-to-hand combat with Linx in episode 4 is undertaken at great risk to himself, so that Sarah and Professor Rubeish can effect the escape of the scientists. The Doctor's heroism is expressed in terms of risk and sacrifice in order to achieve a compassionate objective.

Linx is conceived in heroic terms, but his heroism is opposed to the Doctor even as it is appreciated (if misunderstood) by those who spend most of their time with him. Beyond his dazzling otherworldliness, Linx is dressed in a way which connotes violence, and bluntly too. His domed helmet is reminiscent of the ball and chain supposedly used by mounted warriors to smash the skulls of opposing infantry. He asserts his prowess to Irongron with the threat of force, as shown in the casual way he disposes of Bloodaxe's weapon, but promises benevolence and the gift of advanced weaponry to promote Irongron's cause. Where the Doctor is a teacher and collaborator, Linx positions himself as an idol, to awe. This is one side of his heroic mould, the one he presents to his human hosts. The other is the dedication of a Sontaran officer to return to his fleet and continue the war against the Rutans. One, however, informs the other. Linx professes to be amused by his arming of Irongron[104], but he is also passing on his ethic as well as his

---

[104] Part Two.

weaponry. Linx presents himself as an exemplary warrior, emphasising the enjoyment of war over Irongron's pragmatic reluctance to squander men and weapons.

A scene present in the rehearsal script, but which never reached the studio, suggests that until late in development Linx came close to seeing Irongron as his comrade and expressed a shared soldierly bond. Two pages of dialogue were cut from the scene in episode 4 where Irongron finds Linx where the Doctor has left him, tied up in the workshop, and releases him. Irongron begs Linx to let him raise an army so they can 'march together, among the stars and sack the golden castles of heaven!' Linx replies by recognising Irongron's 'noble, martial spirit,' that Irongron would make a good Sontaran, and that Linx has grown fond of him. This emotional moment interrupts the tension, as Irongron and Linx are both anxious at this point to see the death of the Doctor, and Linx is doubly anxious to leave the planet, and breaks the existing and enduring thread of mutual distance. The performances of Kevin Lindsay and David Daker focused on Linx's humiliation at being reliant on Irongron, and the human's longing for weapons which will give him an unbeatable advantage over his knightly neighbours. This expression of comradeship would have been difficult to carry off in that context. However, had it been included, Irongron's turning on Linx when he realises that his castle really is going to be destroyed would have been an even stronger recognition of betrayal by a false role model.

The Two Scientific Advisers

The appearance of Brigadier Lethbridge-Stewart in episode 1 of *The Time Warrior* might be found superfluous or misleading, as UNIT's command structure plays little part in the first episode and the organisation is entirely absent from the rest of the story. However, the inclusion of Lethbridge-Stewart in the first episode invites the viewer to compare the Doctor's role as adviser to one military figure, with Linx's role as adviser to another.

The Brigadier and Irongron both take advantage of scientific knowledge and skill from outside their world and time. Linx's request for shelter and equipment in episode 1 closely resembles the deal between the Doctor and the Brigadier drawn at the end of *Spearhead from Space*. One crucial difference is that Linx's offer is immediately based on increasing Irongron's offensive capability:

> 'I can give you weapons. Weapons that can make you master, so that none dare stand against you. You shall take what castles you will [...] Weapons that can strike a man dead from far away. You can be supreme warrior.'[105]

In *Spearhead from Space*, it is the Brigadier who defines what he wants from the Doctor: 'If they [the Nestenes] do decide to launch a second attack, I hope we can count on your help again?'[106] In *Spearhead from Space*, the Brigadier never sees the Doctor as a threat, even when he maintains scepticism about his identity. The Brigadier accepts the Doctor is imprisoned by circumstances outside his control and seeks to postpone his departure rather than prevent it. Most importantly, the Brigadier is engaged in defence, not conquest. Irongron is outside the sociopolitical order; the Brigadier is inside it. Irongron threatens Linx as soon as Linx asks for help; he is accustomed to taking what he wants – living by purchase rather

---

[105] Part One.
[106] *Spearhead from Space*, Episode 4.

than by pay, in the manner of Sir Walter Scott's Border freebooters[107] – and thinks in terms of booty, food, men and raw materials above ideas. In the rehearsal script for episode 1, Linx attempts to place Irongron under mind control:

> [LINX POINTS THE TUBE AT IRONGRON. FOR A MOMENT IRONGRON IS TRANSFIXED, THEN HE SHAKES HIMSELF AND RUBS HIS EYES.]
>
> IRONGRON
>
> Do you seek to dazzle me with your treachery?

Only when Irongron proves resistant does Linx bargain, and once Linx has secured space for his workshop he prefers to be left undisturbed by his hosts unless it proves diplomatically necessary.

In contrast, even at his most acerbic, the Doctor likes human company. The nature of his scientific advice reflects this sociability; he is interested in making friends, human or Silurian or alien ambassador, and his early technological efforts are often aimed at identifying or containing problems or establishing dialogue.

Linx's technical advice to Irongron is more transactional. He provides Irongron with a rifle but seems to have given him the most minimal advice on how to use it, leaving Irongron to practise by trial and error. The rehearsal script for episode 1 envisaged Irongron telling Bloodaxe, 'As yet I have not the trick of its use,' followed by the rifle exploding and chipping out some wall, before the recorded sequence where Irongron practises firing at an apple. Where the Doctor engages with his human hosts' concerns, Linx plies his with weapons

---

[107] Scott, Walter, *Minstrelsy of the Scottish Border*, 2nd ed, volume 1, plx.

as distractions and rides with them to the siege of Sir Edward's castle for entertainment. He advises Irongron to use his new rifles, and points out to Irongron that the defenders, impervious to bullets, are dummies. Like Irongron, he seems to have given up in the face of the Doctor's 'special smoking mixture', but blames Irongron entirely for the retreat and begins to hint at his imminent departure. He only advises as long as he is interested.

Linx is not only too selfish to adequately advise Irongron, he's too narrowly focused. His assessment of the Time Lords as '[a] race of great technical achievement, lacking the morale to withstand a determined assault' is perhaps generally remembered as part of Robert Holmes' belittling of the Time Lords, but here betrays a mind which only thinks in terms of military capabilities. Unlike the Doctor, he seems to have little knowledge of other life forms. He is notoriously surprised to find that Sarah Jane Smith is of a 'different species'. In the script for episode 1, he pauses before first mentioning 'men' to Irongron, perhaps a hint at his unfamiliarity with gender. In the rehearsal script for episode 4 it was made plain that he didn't understand that people had to be fed:

DOCTOR

Your prisoners have gone with little food and no rest for days. They are physically exhausted, can't you see?

LINX

They can still work.

DOCTOR

Not for much longer.

They require more protein to turn into energy?

DOCTOR

Exactly. And a chance to sleep.

Perhaps this last exchange was dropped as much because it made Linx look stupid as for timing reasons.

The Doctor throughout demonstrates his broad appreciation of cultural values, telling Sarah in episode 3 about his wish to study art under Rembrandt and comparing his chandelier swing in episode 4 to 'the daring young man on the flying trapeze', on top of his otherworldly scientific knowledge. Linx belittles a species he sees as primitive, but the Doctor wants to protect humanity. The Doctor's interference in defence of the 'course of history' is validated by the authorial decision to let one of the medieval characters, Hal, kill Linx, a privilege given to the Doctor in Holmes' original storyline. The Doctor's role as adviser rather than principal actor in human affairs is confirmed. The pursuit of science prospers when it is at its least selfish.

The Two Magicians

From his first appearance, Linx is associated with the supernatural and with magic. On his emergence from his spacecraft, Linx is recognised by Bloodaxe as 'a devil from hell' before he introduces himself as a Sontaran, leaving Bloodaxe to think him 'a Saracen. I have heard tales of their Eastern magic.' The association with the Saracens recalls Sir Brian de Bois-Guilbert in *Ivanhoe* and his 'wild and outlandish' entourage, which includes two Saracen servants[108], together with the criticism the Templar Grand Master offers of those Templars who study 'the magic of the Paynim Saracens.'[109] The Templars were a crusading order founded in the Holy Land who saw their first home on the Temple Mount in Jerusalem as spiritually and physically close to heaven. Irongron at first supposes Linx to be a 'star warrior', a soldier from the borders of the celestial realm sent as a test; given the time period and that his favourite oath in the rehearsal script seems to be 'by the Cross', it's certainly conceivable that Irongron sees Linx's arrival as a divine challenge which will legitimate his right of pillage and conquest if he is successful. Instead, he makes a pact which has elements of that Faustus made with Mephistopheles in Marlowe's *Doctor Faustus* (1592), but unlike Mephistopheles, who distracts Faustus with what are little more than conjuring tricks, Linx has every intention, for his own amusement and protection, of increasing Irongron's worldly power.

Linx's outer appearance has something of the magician about it. His weapon is not a projectile, but a magic wand with which he can smite a sword from a hand and hypnotise captives into telling him whatever they wish. However, this is a role which he performs with reluctance, largely being anxious to return to his work and dwelling underground almost as if this was his native habitat. Robert Holmes later claimed that he drew aspects of *The Time Warrior* from Norse mythology, specifically mentioning the name Irongron[110]. While there seems to be no Norse antecedent for Irongron – Bloodaxe, however, recalling the Viking last king of Northumbria, Erik Bloodaxe

---

[108] Scott, *Ivanhoe*, Book I, chapter 2.
[109] Scott, *Ivanhoe*, Book III, chapter 5.
[110] *The Complete* History #20, p99.

(d.954) – Linx's preference for his underground cave-like lair recalls the trolls of Scandinavian mythology. Linx's skin tones are close to the colour of the stone walls at the location, Peckforton Castle, suggesting that within the armour is a creature who has been magicked out of the fabric of the castle itself. The clay-like appearance of the Sontarans was adopted by Ian Marter in his novelisation of the second Sontaran serial, where he had Harry Sullivan think the Sontaran officer Styr (sic) was 'like the statue of a huge, thick-limbed man somehow brought to life' which 'looks like the Golem', 'the man-made effigy brought to life by means of the Shem, the magic charm, destruction of which would render the creature lifeless again'[111]. Marter responded to the appearance of the Sontarans by drawing on Jewish folklore rather than Norse mythology or British literary precedents for Linx, but his choices reflected the layers of the supernatural costume design had added to Linx in *The Time Warrior* and thus to succeeding Sontarans.

News of Linx's sorcery spreads even though Linx is not seen outside Irongron's castle. In episode 2, Sir Edward has already heard reports of 'devils and magicians' working with Irongron, even before Hal tells him of his encounter with the robot knight. Sarah denies that the Doctor is a magician – 'Just some eccentric scientist' – but her explanation that she comes from 'somewhere where they have a kind of science that would seem like magic to you' only confirms Edward's belief that he is facing 'madness, sorcery and witchcraft!' When Eleanor describes Sarah's 'scientists [...] learned men' as 'these wizards', she confirms that *The Time Warrior* is drawing upon a theme already established in Barry Letts' producership, that of Arthur C Clarke's 'Third Law': 'Any sufficiently advanced technology

---

[111] Marter, *The Sontaran Experiment* pp45, 54.

is indistinguishable from magic'[112], as already demonstrated in *The Dæmons*. The conduct of the Doctor as magician in *The Time Warrior* inverts this notion, and presents conjuring and the accoutrements of television 'special effects' as high technology. The Doctor directs the defence of the castle in episode 3 by dummies who are inanimate and therefore invulnerable to Linx's weapons (a parody of Linx's unbeatable robot knight), and assembles his 'special smoking mixture of saltpetre, sulphur and fat' 'a superior sort of stink bomb'. Saltpetre and sulphur were ingredients of early gunpowder and it is conceivable that Sir Edward would have held stocks of them. Scientific advice and magic blend: in episode 4, the sleeping mixture which Sarah adds to the food consumed by Irongron and his men is 'scientifically' prepared by the Doctor and effected with subterfuge rather than incantations, but the principle is familiar to the audience from fairy tales.

It's unsurprising that a medieval story should involve at least comparisons of science with magic, given the magical content in the Arthurian legends, some traces of which remain in *The Time Warrior*. The sickly Sir Edward recalls the Fisher King of Arthurian legend, unable to heal from a severe wound. Indeed, the rehearsal script for episode 1 makes it explicit in introductory dialogue that Edward has brought back a 'wasting sickness' from the Crusades – which Edward surely regards as a holy war. Edward also resembles the King Arthur of several medieval romances, whose fighting days are behind him and who rarely stirs from his (admittedly travelling) court, and who instead plays host to younger men who undertake heroic deeds, the parallel in that case Hal the archer. Edward then seeks a Merlin in the

---

[112] Clarke, Arthur C, 'Clarke's Third Law on UFOs', *Science*, new ser, vol. 159, no 3812, 19 January 1968.

Doctor. There are several aspects of Merlin as seen in 19th and 20th-century literature and popular culture in the Doctor. His practicality and subterfuge are reminiscent of the Merlin of **The Adventures of Sir Lancelot**, but his relationship to time is closer to the Merlin of TH White's Arthurian cycle, collected as *The Once and Future King* (1958). The Victorian Merlin has been characterised as helpless in the thrall of the sexual power of Vivien, the pupil who betrays and imprisons him. The nearest parallel is the asexual Linx, who captures the investigating Doctor in his dungeon with the intention of draining him of his secrets, and indeed in one poem (by R Macleod Fullarton, 1890), Vivien specifically seeks both feminine and masculine forms of power, declaring she shall 'be King!'[113]

Perhaps the most intriguing Arthurian precedent is in Mark Twain's *A Connecticut Yankee in King Arthur's Court* (1889). There, Hank Morgan, a factory superintendent from late 19th-century Connecticut, is transported to the court of King Arthur, realises he has greater scientific knowledge than anyone in the kingdom, and begins a series of reforms both establishing his authority and introducing selected people to the tools of the industrial age, including modern weapons such as several different types of gun. Twain has Morgan rhapsodise about one of his pupils being examined:

> 'It was beautiful to hear the lad lay out the science of war, and wallow in details of battle and siege, of supply, transportation, mining and countermining, grand tactics, big strategy and little strategy, signal service, infantry, cavalry, artillery, and all

[113] Barczewski, Stephanie L., *Myth and National Identity in Nineteenth-century Britain* pp179-180

about siege guns, field guns, gatling guns, rifled guns, smooth bores, musket practice, revolver practice...'[114]

Morgan anticipates Linx's praise of warfare and his gifts of percussion weapons to Irongron. Bearing the title of 'the Boss' and with his uncritical pursuit of mechanisation and the reorganisation of Arthurian Britain around the high technology of his own day without regard for the consequences, Twain's protagonist also suggests an influence on the Doctor's computer antagonist, BOSS, in the preceding story to *The Time Warrior*, *The Green Death*.

Hank Morgan was once widely taken to be Twain's hero. The principal targets of Twain were traditionally identified as inherited privilege, superstition and the Catholic Church, with Morgan's technological revolution threatening to overturn a society blinded by rank and crippled by gentility. However, more recent scholarship recognises Twain's relationship with the medieval as more complicated, typified in scenes such as that where Morgan disguises himself in plate armour to render himself less conspicuous, just as Holmes envisaged Linx would in his storyline[115]. Morgan is also forced to resort to the character of a magician in spite of himself, much as Linx is frustrated and wearied by the superstitious explanations Irongron and his men have for his technology, and as the Doctor denies that his magic has any supernatural basis. Twain's novel ends with Morgan and his allies inflicting on each other the same kind of terrible mass slaughter which the Doctor believes will be the inevitable result of Linx's involvement in human history.

---

[114] Twain, Mark, *A Connecticut Yankee in King Arthur's Court*, Chapter 25.
[115] Twain, *Connecticut Yankee* Chapter 11; Molesworth, *Robert Holmes*, p206.

Morgan's faith that he embodies reason and his references to the need for violent revolution or aggressive colonisation to achieve change anticipate the imperialism of force which underlies Linx's technological magic[116].

The Doctor is not immune from criticism through the lens of Hank Morgan: his 'superior smoking mixture' is much the same sort of effect as both Morgan and Merlin (believed, in the final analysis erroneously, to be a complete charlatan by Morgan) use in their competition to restore the Holy Fountain[117]. The difference lies in what their condescension hides. The Boss' attempt to lead an anachronistic revolution ends in a prophecy of future war. The Doctor's failure to side with the rebels, criminal and murderous as they are, is endorsed by the harmonious relationship between the ineffectual Edward, his assertive wife Eleanor, and their loyal bowman Hal (and in the rehearsal script Mary, who is both Eleanor's attendant and Hal's lover). When Edward says he will take no part in a duel between sorcerers, he is distancing himself from both magic and the possibility of changing history by supernatural means; after all, in seeking divine aid to overthrow Islamic domination in the Middle East, he has already tried and been punished for it. The way forward is consensual, imaginative and compassionate.

Perhaps, though, it's the 1949 musical film version of *A Connecticut Yankee in King Arthur's Court* which has more direct relation to *The*

---

[116] For a discussion of Hank Morgan as an expression of Mark Twain's questioning of the Enlightenment values he at first set out to champion in *A Connecticut Yankee*, see Hasty, Will, 'Revolutions and Final Solutions: On Enlightenment and its Dialectic in Mark Twain's *A Connecticut Yankee in King Arthur's Court*', *Arthuriana* 24:2, 2014.
[117] Twain, *Connecticut Yankee* Chapters 22-23.

Time Warrior. Tay Garnett's picture is much more relaxed about the romanticisation of the past than Twain ever was. BBC schedulers might have recognised the parallels, scheduling the film for a 3pm transmission on BBC Two on Saturday 29 December 1973, a few hours before the broadcast of episode 3 of *The Time Warrior* on BBC One[118].

The **Doctor Who** of the early 1970s preached rationalism, like Hank Morgan, but like the 1949 film's Hank Martin (Bing Crosby, a performer who inhabited a similar career space to Jon Pertwee) had fewer illusions about what it could achieve. Martin changes individuals rather than society, including rousing King Arthur (here played by Cedric Hardwicke) from lassitude and ill-health into an interest in the betterment of his people, much as the Doctor and Sarah show Sir Edward how he can resist Irongron. Although here it is magic, put to ill use in the hands of the evil Merlin, which wins the day, there remains a promise of a better world in Hank Martin's present. This is presented as a romantic possibility in the person of a young woman who looks just like Martin's Arthurian love Lady Alysande (Rhonda Fleming), whereas in *The Time Warrior* the better world appears in the actions of the Doctor and Sarah, who use the resources of the Middle Ages to upend Linx's sorcery and let it destroy itself. The Doctor is a magician despite his denials, and is recognised as such by Sarah, because he has upheld the values of her present without compromising the past and done so with a preponderance of wit and charm over violence. These were spells as valued by an America adjusting to an enhanced world role in the 1940s, as by a Britain seeking to project a status beyond its

---

[118] 'Saturday Cinema: A Connecticut Yankee in King Arthur's Court', *BBC Genome*.

diminished condition in the early 1970s.

A note running through the serial invites one more comparison with a cinema musical. Linx's method of time travel involves an 'osmic projector'. 'Osmic' is an adjective referring to compounds of the element osmium, often used as fixatives in microscopy; or, a more likely inspiration for Holmes given his predilection for mentioning foul smells in **Doctor Who** scripts, 'of or relating to the sense of smell' or even 'the branch of science concerned with odours and the sense of smell'[119]. It's also one 'c' short of 'cosmic', so sounds vaguely space-age. It could also pertain to Oz, as known to most television viewers from the MGM film *The Wizard of Oz* (1939). Although not shown on British television until Christmas Day 1975, it was familiar not only from multiple cinema releases but from stage productions and radio and television adaptations using all or some of the songs and story. Sydney Newman's notes on the first version of **Doctor Who**'s first episode, 'An Unearthly Child', in 1963 had urged that the Doctor be more like Frank Morgan (playing Professor Marvel/the Wizard) in *The Wizard of Oz* – emphasising that the character was more kindly than Hartnell had initially played him but also something of a charlatan. The image of the Wizard is a projection, operated by a man behind a curtain. Sarah entering the TARDIS to expose the Doctor as the kidnapper of the missing scientists is something of a curtain-drawing moment, but with a different result. Linx projects a great and powerful image of himself as warrior-benefactor to Irongron, and like the Wizard in the film, principally wants to return home. Of the two wizards, it's Linx who is more of the charlatan, as behind the Doctor's curtain is the magical science of the TARDIS and the fulfilment of promises. Where Linx projects terror, the Doctor

---

[119] Oxford English Dictionary

embodies and practises benign wizardry and has the ability and inclination to take Sarah Jane Smith – *The Time Warrior*'s questing Dorothy – home.

Clash of Civilisations: Britain, America, and the Brain Drain

> '[The prime minister, Sir Alec Douglas-Home] could offer to let America keep the Beatles if they will leave us Dr Who.'[120]

The research centre seen in episode 1 of *The Time Warrior* draws from Britain's post-imperial crisis following the Second World War. Britain's postwar policy-making was entirely overshadowed by its relations with the United States of America. Friendly relations with the USA were essential to defence, to the economy and to the maintenance of Britain's position as a great power. These realities were already apparent in the middle of the Second World War, but were hard to acknowledge for generations who had either grown up at the sunset of Queen Victoria's imperial reign, or seen the British Empire survive the First World War with an increase in territory. Harold Macmillan, as a cabinet minister in Winston Churchill's government, told future Labour minister Richard Crossman that 'We [...] are Greeks in this American empire,' envisaging Britons as people of higher cultural achievements than the Americans – 'big, vulgar, bustling people, more vigorous than we are and also more idle, with more unspoiled virtues but also more corrupt' – whom British ministers must guide as Macmillan recalled Greek slaves had guided

---

[120] Government Spokesman, 'Government Cannot Stop "Brain Drain"', *The Daily Telegraph*, 12 February 1964.

the Emperor Claudius[121]. Macmillan was fond of repeating the analogy and did so to the Conservative Party's 1922 Committee, its forum for backbench members of the House of Commons, on 22 November 1956, as part of a speech where he stirred a despondent party in the wake of the government's disastrous attempt to seize the Suez Canal from Egypt, and emerged as a serious candidate to succeed discredited prime minister Sir Anthony Eden, who left office seven weeks later[122].

While Macmillan's policy of intensifying Britain's alliance with the USA and gaining more benefits from it had some success, for example on nuclear co-operation, his analogy with the Greeks advising Romans at the heart of their empire was perhaps more true than he intended, as British industry and government found itself unable to stop the emigration of those with much needed scientific and technical skills. On 11 February 1964, a few months after Macmillan left office, Quintin Hogg, who had been minister for science throughout Macmillan's premiership, acknowledged that the USA, 'with a national income eight times our own, could and always would be able to offer facilities, standards of living and salaries beyond the British capacity.'[123] Three years later Hogg claimed that '4,000 British scientists and 350 doctors leave these shores and cross the Atlantic every year.'[124] This consciousness of a loss of talent, a

---

[121] Sampson, *Macmillan: A Study in Ambiguity*; in turn quoted in Ashton, Nigel J, 'Harold Macmillan and the "Golden Days" of Anglo-American Relations Revisited, 1957-63', *Diplomatic History*, Volume 29, Issue 4, 1 September 2005, pp691-723.
[122] Howard, Anthony, *RAB: The Life of R A Butler*, pp240-41.
[123] *The Daily Telegraph*, 12 February 1964.
[124] Parliamentary Debates (Hansard), House of Commons, 13 February 1967, col 126.

symptom of national decline, shapes the conceptualisation and presentation of the research centre and its scientists in *The Time Warrior* and the story's treatment of ideas of civilisation.

In the camera script and on broadcast, the research centre is defined in terms of security and secrecy rather than scientific purpose. 'This place is just about the most top secret research establishment in the country. Most of their work's so secret they don't know what they're doing themselves,' says the Brigadier in episode 1, adding, 'It's also one of the best guarded places in the country. Security details, alarm systems.' The Brigadier goes on to mention 'Space hardware. New alloys, guidance systems, methods of propulsion,' which makes the centre obviously attractive to Linx. However, the rehearsal script contains extra detail which reveals more about the contemporary anxieties which fuelled the adventure. There, the line reads:

> 'Space hardware. Close co-operation with NASA. New alloys, guidance systems, methods of propulsion. We provide the know how, they help to foot the bill. Ministers having kittens.'

Not only is the research centre explicitly linked to NASA, then widely associated with the moon landings and thus the real-life exploration of space rarely mentioned in **Doctor Who** following *The Ambassadors of Death* (1970), but the USA is paying a share of the research centre's costs. Linx's intervention has political and diplomatic consequences.

It's possible that contradiction with *The Ambassadors of Death* led to the removal of the link to NASA. *Ambassadors* had presented a near-future Britain technologically advanced enough to have its own space programme[125], while the rehearsal script for *The Time Warrior* depicted a Britain closer to that in the newspaper headlines, afflicted by financial crises and uncertain about how it could embrace a changing world. Alternatively, the change promoted a more general constructive ambiguity about when the UNIT stories were set. This note was always present in the '(near-)contemporary' Earth stories, but intensified once design guidelines for UNIT and its environment pulled back from the futuristic in the 1971 season, and time and space travel made its return to **Doctor Who**. For example, In episode 2 of *Day of the Daleks*, the viewer joins a conversation between the Controller and Jo Grant, where the Controller remarks 'You've told me the year' from which Jo has come to the 22nd century, information to which the viewer is not privy. A change between both rehearsal and camera scripts on one hand, and broadcast on the other, comes in episode 2 of *The Time Warrior* where, interrogated under hypnosis by Linx, Sarah reveals which time she comes from. On broadcast, this is a short exchange:

LINX

Which century?

SARAH

Twentieth.

The equivalent in the camera and rehearsal scripts contains the same number of syllables, but is different:

---

[125] Discussed in Myles, LM, *The Black Archive #3: The Ambassadors of Death*, pp63-73.

LINX

Time?

SARAH

Nineteen seventy four.[126]

Aside from setting a precedent which might have avoided or further complicated what fandom would term the 'UNIT dating controversy', the revised exchange preserves the sense of playfulness which allows the prime minister to be called Jeremy (in *The Green Death*) and the government to be funding research into the transition of matter through interstitial time (*The Time Monster*) while the cast wear contemporary fashions and make occasional pop culture references appropriate for the year of broadcast. The effect, though, when applied to the script for *The Time Warrior*, is to draw the venom from the author's satirical sting.

Nevertheless, a parallel remains in that Linx is effecting a brutal parody of the 'brain drain'. NASA's subsidy of the research centre, as reported by the Brigadier, had turned scientists into a form of invisible export, as they remained in Britain but were benefiting a US government agency. Linx makes them invisible by removing them from the research centre. As characterised by the Brigadier in the rehearsal script, the scientists are domesticated people rather than adventurous, a scientist having gone into his bathroom to clean his teeth, witnessed by his wife, who found the bathroom empty minutes later, with toothbrush on the floor, the tap running and the window, the only means of exit, locked from the inside. Irongron

---

[126] *The Time Warrior*, Part Two (rehearsal and camera scripts), scene 1, p9.

would probably judge them as 'whey-faced ninnies'[127] even without Linx's hypnotism.

The most ninnyish of all, on surface appearances, is Professor Rubeish. His name is an obvious pun, spotted in probably the first fan review of the story by Doctor Who Fan Club organiser Keith Miller – 'what sounded […] like a joke from Morecambe and Wise.'[128] He is unapologetically introduced in the rehearsal script as 'RUBBISH, A SCIENTIST' and at least once appears as 'RUBEITH' as if Robert Holmes and Terrance Dicks were uncertain how modestly the script's unsubtlety should be cloaked. He's apparently happy to withdraw from the world, regarding the absence of his wife and family as 'a silver lining', drifts away from conversation with the Doctor and Sarah to write equations on the door of the TARDIS, and behaves as the audience might expect an absent-minded professor to do. He seems designed for the audience to contrast with the Doctor and Sarah, who are broad-minded, adventurously interested in the world beyond them, and display competence through outward confidence.

However, it is wrong to write off Rubeish. He is so visually impaired that he can't be hypnotised by Linx, but has enough guile to escape detection. His myopia is accompanied by a stubbornness and an inventiveness, as seen by his manufacture of his lorgnette eyepiece to help his vision. He's neither interested nor capable enough to join the Doctor in his successive escapes from Linx's workshop, but monitors events as best he can and in part 4 plays a decisive role by unhypnotising the scientists and managing their return to the 20th century by osmic projector. He lacks the energy and inquisitiveness

---

[127] Part Three.
[128] Miller, Keith, *DWFC Mag* 19, January 1974, reprinted in *The Official Doctor Who Fan Club volume 1: The Jon Pertwee Years*, p186.

of the Doctor, or the vigour and viciousness of Linx or Irongron, but he is able to provide specific skills when required and perhaps even has his mind opened, realising that he misses home comforts. His tweediness is a stereotypically academic look, but it has something of the costume of the country gentleman adopted when prime minister by Harold Macmillan. If Linx is in part a caricature of American militarism, then Rubeish is a caricature of Macmillan's Britons as enslaved Greeks, submerged in an empire which is not their own but still able to impart their wisdom. If so, it's a double-edged comment; while Rubeish has his gifts, most of his colleagues have lost their individuality to become 'zombie' workers, and he can barely see. If Rubeish does represent post-imperial Britain, then he is very vulnerable and needs external help to make him realise and overcome his predicament.

The Two Aliens

The external help to post-imperial Britain has of course come from the Doctor. That the Doctor comes from somewhere other than Earth isn't something *The Time Warrior* feels it needs to stress as much as earlier first stories of a season in Jon Pertwee's time had done. *Spearhead from Space*, *Terror of the Autons* and *The Three Doctors* (1972-3) had all foregrounded the Doctor's alienness, whether as newly-transformed hospital patient with a non-human metabolism, as counterpart to the newly-arrived Master, or as being from another world joined by two people who were actually earlier versions of himself. In episode 1 of *Day of the Daleks*, the Doctor expresses a lack of interest in politics, not just because he is a 'scientist, not a politician,' but because 'humans are always squabbling over something.' His gestures suggest a concession to the seriousness of the crisis once the Brigadier has persuaded him that a world war is imminent, but he proceeds to treat his investigation with a degree of nonchalance, proceeding through the larder of supposedly haunted Auderly House 'like a one-man food and wine society'. In contrast, the Doctor of *The Time Warrior* seems vastly more relaxed when we meet him at the research centre. In narrative terms, he is now on Earth by choice rather than as an exile. Practically, maintaining conflict with the Brigadier would undermine the Brigadier's role as friend and confidant; there is no longer a Jo Grant to whom the Doctor can vent his frustration with the military mind. Indeed, in episode 1 when Professor Rubeish complains about the Brigadier, calling him a 'military idiot', the Doctor mounts a non-confrontational defence: 'I know how you feel. Still, he means well.'

For the third Doctor, as for the majority of televised **Doctor Who**, Earth means Britain, and usually London or nearby in southern England. This is largely true for 21st century **Doctor Who**, even when those areas are (as often since 2005) depicted by Cardiff or elsewhere in South Wales. The Doctor and **Doctor Who** have often been characterised by professionals and critics alike as representative of a particular Britishness. Despite the scripted lines which mark the third Doctor as an outsider, he was notoriously viewed by Verity Lambert (**Doctor Who**'s producer from 1963-65) as an 'establishment figure [...] getting on the 'phone to the Prime Minister every five minutes.'[129]

The first book-length academic study of **Doctor Who**, *Doctor Who: The Unfolding Text* (1983), discussed with the programme's production teams the character and the programme's British identity and apparent establishment outlook in terms of cultural and

---

[129] *The Guardian*, 23 June 1972.

economic differences between British and American television and the institutional outlook of the BBC. For Philip Hinchcliffe, who produced **Doctor Who** for three seasons from the one which followed *The Time Warrior,* the Doctor was British because he was 'a bit rough around the edges', not 'a wonderfully logical worked out "quirky" hero who was always the same'[130], accommodating the kinds of shift in characterisation described in the last paragraph within the practical requirements of BBC television craft rather than the advertising-led US model. Comparably, what the authors of *The Unfolding Text* saw as the programme's 'liberal-populist' 'sceptical, aggressive ironic and detached qualities', critical of all forms of extremism, arose from what Terrance Dicks called 'a kind of realism' addressed to how people lived their lives in the 1970s, and what Barry Letts acknowledged was the default 'liberal/left of centre' position of a collective of intelligent people, which *The Unfolding Text* understood as his characterisation of the BBC[131]. Writing in the early 1980s, the third Doctor could be looked back on as representative of a particular BBC Britishness which took advantage of his institutional position – whether in the BBC or UNIT – to negotiate or impose a moderate consensus which reconciled competing interests.

Subsequent to *The Unfolding Text*, and with the consensual BBC of Letts and Dicks receding into history, the third Doctor has been characterised as less liberal and more specifically national in character. Piers Britton and Simon Barker draw on Britton's 1994

---

[130] Tulloch, John and Manuel Alvarado, *Doctor Who: The Unfolding Text,* pp178.

[131] Tulloch and Alvarado, *The Unfolding Text*, pp52-54

interview with Pertwee in claiming he 'played the Doctor as an implacable ultra-English hero in the Bulldog Drummond mould'[132]. For James Chapman the Doctor's perpetual tinkering with gadgetry and impatience with authority is reminiscent of a perhaps more globally recognisable figure of England or (given the Scottish influences upon his creation) Great Britain, Sherlock Holmes, whose authority was expressed with greater eccentricity than Drummond[133]. Alec Charles locates the Doctor as an expression of the contradictions within post-war late British imperialism, whose benevolent interventions in intergalactic crises reinstate 'the very imperialist agendas and alibis which [the Doctor] purports to oppose'[134].

The Doctor's alienness is partly an expression of the liberal consensus from which the production team of the day made **Doctor Who**, and of its attempt to accommodate late imperial anxieties concerning Britain's historic world role and challenges to assumptions concerning it. The perpetuation of British military power, now deployed against extraterrestrial (or subterranean) threats under the direction of a United Nations agency, played in to a postwar interest in 'world government' which sought to internationalise the perceived benefits of empire. It was a favoured aspiration of Clement Attlee, Labour prime minister from 1945 to

---

[132] Britton, Piers D, and Simon J Barker, *Reading Between Designs: Visual Imagery and the Generation of Meaning in The Avengers, The Prisoner and Doctor Who*, p149.

[133] Chapman, James, *Inside the TARDIS: The Worlds of Doctor Who*, 2nd ed, p78.

[134] Charles, Alec, 'The Ideology of Anachronism' in Butler, *Time And Relative Dissertations In Space*, p117.

1951, one he particularly articulated in later life in the 1960s[135]. The United Nations policy on 'trust territories' – confiscated from defeated colonial powers in two world wars – was shot through with language which assumed the primacy of European civilisation, in practical terms the civilisations of Britain and France. Discussion of the peoples of trust territories in the postwar period included a 1955 article which described Tanganyika in 1920 as possessing 'a type of subsistence economy which was just reaching the monetary stage'[136], and which government by Britain under the League of Nations mandate and United Nations trusteeship had brought to economic prosperity, if not literacy and democracy.

When the Doctor implores Linx to understand that 'Human beings have **got** to be allowed to develop at their own pace. At this period, they're just a few steps away from barbarism,'[137] he's echoing this European attitude towards colonial territories. The argument that non-European countries should 'develop at their own pace' was not exclusively that of Europeans disparaging colonialism. It's sufficiently general to appeal to several strands of thought in 1970s Britain: the advocates of 'separate development', sympathetic to the apartheid regime in South Africa or Ian Smith's government in Rhodesia, as well as those who supported African self-determination with minimal involvement from anyone of European descent. The Doctor could plausibly appear as the representative of a pan-human consensus

---

[135] 'Clement Attlee at 80 – archive, 1963', *The Guardian,* 3 January 2017 (3 January 1963); *Parliamentary Debates (Hansard), House of Commons,* 23 October 1967, vol 751 cc1355-67.
[136] Bates, Margaret L, 'Tanganyika: The Development of a Trust Territory' *International Organization* 9:1, February 1955.
[137] Part Two (camera script).

against destructive exploitation where being 'not ready' is a feint to make use of colonialist prejudice as much as an acceptance of a ruling model of progress. His conversations with Linx are all statements of principle allied with attempts to meet Linx halfway. The Doctor's attempts to negotiate a non-disruptive solution to Linx's plight, like his anecdotes of his diplomacy at an intergalactic peace conference told in *Frontier in Space*, draw on the cosmopolitanism manifest in his impatience with Little Englanders, the unimaginative, and those who can't see that appreciating a fine wine or a well-matured cheese isn't an obstacle to getting a job done. In that sense, he breaks with some (but not all) archetypes of the British hero. He's not inclined to make any assumptions about superiority.

In the rehearsal script for episode 3, the Doctor flippantly attributes Irongron's attack on him to 'acute xenalasia [sic][...] That was the old Spartan custom, you know, of driving aliens from the country.' Later in the same episode, as broadcast, the Doctor rejects Sarah's question 'My species? You talk as if you weren't human!' with 'Yes, well, the definition of the word humanity was always a rather a complex question, wasn't it?'[138] While acknowledging that he is not 'a native of the planet Terra,' the Doctor has made his point. He is an alien within Sarah's definition, but his talking of the Time Lords as 'my people' doesn't prevent him taking up the cause of Sarah's. His cultured, multifaceted universalism has analogies in several leading

---

[138] In the rehearsal script Sarah's line is a more doubtful 'You talk as if you weren't − human?' as part of a longer exchange. In both rehearsal and camera scripts the Doctor responds with the more condescending 'The definition of humanity is a somewhat complex question, my dear.'

figures in British postwar life who were exiles from their countries of origin, but had established successful and versatile careers in the UK, such as the publisher George Weidenfeld or the literary agent Harvey Unna, whose clients included Terrance Dicks and who was cited by another client, Michael Bond, as an influence on the creation of Paddington Bear[139].

The Doctor's cosmopolitanism is accompanied by an urbane willingness to emphasise what he has in common with others. Where he emphasises his otherworldliness to Linx, it's his appreciation of courtesy which he stresses to Sir Edward and Lady Eleanor when introduced to them in episode 3. While the Doctor's flattery of Edward and Eleanor – 'It is a pleasure and a privilege to be in the company of civilised people at last'[140] – can be read as the Doctor's embrace of the 'civilised' values of the conquering 'Norman' class over those of 'barbarous', 'primitive', 'Anglo-Saxon' Irongron, the Doctor's association with Edward and Eleanor is not an uncomplicated embrace of developmental 'stagism'[141]. It's just as much someone attempting to defuse potential hostility by establishing a more effective social strategy than he managed at Irongron's castle. In accommodating the values of his captors, the Doctor is repeating a strategy seen in Holmes' previous story, *Carnival of Monsters*, where his 'Hello. Topping day, what?' to Major

---

[139] Pick, Hella, 'Lord Weidenfeld Obituary', *The Guardian*, 20 January 2016; 'Harvey Unna', *The Times,* 5 August 2003; Reuben, Susan 'Paddington Bear: His Secret Jewish Heritage', *thejc.com*, 29 June 2017.

[140] The 'at last' is not in the script.

[141] As might be understood from Orthia, Lindy A, 'Savages, Science, Stagism, and the Naturalized Ascendancy of the Not-We in **Doctor Who**', in Orthia, Lindy, ed, *Doctor Who and Race*, p281.

Daly and Claire in episode 1 is a short-term attempt to deflect their curiosity and effect his and Jo's escape. Material lost from the rehearsal script for episode 3 would also have emphasised Sir Edward's timidity, a poor advertisement for civilised values:

> 'Irongron has many times our force Hal. We must leave at once [...] If we go south through the forest we may win safe to my Lord of Salisbury's castle. He will give us refuge.'

While the Doctor finds it easier to ally with largely benevolent authority figures such as Sir Edward (or the Brigadier), his position as an outsider to Earth and indeed to the chronological progression of time means he maintains a critical distance and level of disassociation: there is no farewell to Edward and Eleanor at the end of the story, whose purpose (for plot and the Doctor) has been served.

Linx as Alien

Linx's physical distinctiveness makes it much harder for him to blend in with his new environment than the Doctor. His Sontaran space armour is sufficiently similar to that of the society in which he is stranded that he complements his surroundings but remains distinct from them. There are segments in the rehearsal scripts left over from an earlier version where he was still wearing human armour. In that for episode 1, Irongron urges Linx to 'Raise your visor!' and a curious stage direction, 'LINX REPLACES HIS HELMENT' (*sic*), appears after Linx has 'unlocked' the mind of Eric, Sir Edward's messenger, suggesting that the memorable 'suspended enigma' of Linx unveiling his alien features as the cliffhanger to episode 1 only emerged late in development, or that there would be a build up suggesting that Linx's victims had to see his face to be hypnotised, recalling both the hypnotic power of the Master (established in Holmes' *Terror of the Autons*) and anticipating the optically-printed glowing mesmeric eyes of Li H'sen Chang (in another Holmes story, *The Talons of Weng-Chiang* (1977)). The emphasis on 'AN AQUEDUCT, PART OF THE CASTLE'S DRAINAGE SYSTEM' as a feature of Linx's workshop is present in the rehearsal script for episode 1, but apart from one use by the Doctor to enter the workshop through the watercourse's access grille in episode 2 it doesn't play the prominent role one might expect onscreen. Perhaps its inclusion was tied into Linx's appearance if that was intended to be more explicitly amphibian and toad-like.

One of the important details in Linx's armour is the probic vent. This would become part of **Doctor Who**'s mythology, instrumental in the deaths or injuries of Sontarans in *The Invasion of Time* and *The Sontaran Stratagem / The Poison Sky* (2008). As broadcast, *The Time Warrior* does not explain what the probic vent is for. It's only explicitly stated onscreen that Sontarans are fed through it in *The Sontaran Stratagem*, but there is enough in *The Sontaran Experiment* for the audience to infer it. In episode 2 the Doctor warns Harry that Styre is vulnerable at the back of his neck, not long before the Doctor instructs Harry how to sabotage the device in the Sontaran spacecraft through which Styre feeds on 'pure energy'. The two Sontaran novelisations published in 1978 added further details. Robert Holmes in his prologue to *Doctor Who and the Time Warrior* describes Linx drawing energy from his spacecraft through 'a probic insertion in the trapezius' while Ian Marter had Harry discover two more Sontarans attached to an 'Energiser Unit' inside Styr's ship[142].

The explanation in the rehearsal script is at variance with what would be established subsequently. In episode 3, following the flight of Linx with Irongron and his troops from Sir Edward's castle, the Doctor and Sarah celebrate with Sir Edward's household on a grander scale than seen on television. True to the image of the connoisseur of food and wine established in *Day of the Daleks*, the Doctor reflects that his enjoyment of a chicken leg and Sir Edward's wine is 'a pleasure poor old Linx will never know', explaining to Sarah that 'Sontarans don't eat. Or drink either come to that [...] They have a small filter at the base of the neck called the probic vent. It absorbs nutrient from the atmosphere and converts it directly into energy.' Sarah objects that 'It's only like whales and plankton,' again suggesting that the Sontarans were conceived as vaguely aquatic creatures. The rehearsal script for episode 4 has the Doctor describe the vent (to Linx, but in Rubeish's hearing) as 'that small yellow square at the back of your neck', perhaps also suggesting a greenish colour scheme for Linx's form. By the camera script, and on transmission, the vent is 'that small hole at the back of your neck', recognising that its realisation was more brutalist and less futuristic or organic than was visualised at scripting stage.

Linx's physical realisation is functional, and so is his philosophy. The goals of the Sontarans and the Sontaran Empire are supreme and must be pursued with maximum efficiency. There are indications in the rehearsal script that Linx's ambitions might have been developed more thoroughly in an earlier draft. The exchanges between the

---

[142] Dicks, *The Time Warrior,* p10; Marter, *The Sontaran Experiment,* p112.

Doctor and Linx over Linx's plans can read as if they are referring to speeches which have already been deleted, but they are still fuller than what reached the camera script and then the screen. In formally annexing Earth to the Sontaran Empire, Linx has contextualised the planet much as a European explorer claimed territories on other continents and then relegated them to an appropriate position for the service of the Empire – which is not at all. As Linx says in episode 2: 'This primitive planet and its affairs are of no importance' compared to 'the glorious war that is my destiny'. Earth 'has no military value. It is of no strategic significance.' In the rehearsal script Linx dismisses the kidnapped scientists as 'Shambling unskilled idiots'. Linx has 'no interest in human evolution', a term introduced by the Doctor – it must be presumed that the Doctor means technological, social and cultural evolution rather than biological, for as he says in the transmitted episode 2, 'At this period they're just a few steps from barbarism [...] They'll have atomic weapons by the 17th century! They'll have the capability to destroy their own planet before they're civilised enough to handle it.' There, the Doctor emphasises his non-interventionist anticolonialism, open as it is to a 'stagist' reading, and the assumption that a collective psychological maturation accompanies technological advances. Even Sarah concurs in the rehearsal script with the Doctor's assertion that 20th-century humanity was able to manage the consequences of the discovery of atomic power: 'Just about – it was touch and go for a while'[143].

Debatably the attitude of Linx undermines the Doctor's own arguments. At the climax to episode 3, Linx dismisses the Doctor's propositions that he has caused 'harm' by kidnapping innocent

---

[143] Part Three.

people, supporting the 'evil and wicked' Irongron, and introducing 'advanced weapons into a society too primitive to cope with them' by shooting the Doctor. Linx comes from a spacefaring civilisation with limited powers of time travel, and if the Doctor's case is followed through should have the maturity to acknowledge the destruction which he is causing. If he does, he chooses not to. In the rehearsal script to episode 4, he falls back on ideology with a limited element of non sequiturs:

LINX

I am a Commander in the Sontaran Army Space Corps.

DOCTOR

So you keep saying.

LINX

I owe these primitives nothing. My concern is to rejoin our glorious struggle for freedom.

DOCTOR

That's such a familiar tune, Linx. But there's no such thing as a super-race.

LINX

Ha! Then we are all equal? Sontarans, Rutans, Time Lords, and the primitives of this planet?

DOCTOR

I didn't say that. I say that no one race has the right to interfere with any other. Then – ultimately – we may all be equal.

> Your Time Lord philosophy is egalitarian twaddle! It is
> weakness!

At which point the Doctor alerts Rubeish to the location of the probic vent and Linx is knocked unconscious.

The oddity is that Linx never says that the Sontarans are a super-race directly. This might be one reason why the line was lost. The rehearsal script reportedly arose from edits made by Terrance Dicks over a weekend after director Alan Bromly expressed his horror at the script he was given when he joined the production, thinking it unrealisable[144]. On the other hand, it's a fair inference given that Linx keeps stating his rank and army as if this explains all his actions. For the audience of 1973 'super-race' meant Nazi Germany in particular, and perhaps also Imperial Japan where a vocal conservative element in society considered the Japanese people, not only the emperor, to be descended from the gods. However, for many of the older audience the 'super-race' would have reminded them of confidence about British or 'Anglo-Saxon' superiority and myths of empire. The Doctor's charges could be made against several imperial powers. Linx's alienness, like that of **Doctor Who**'s most successful unearthly creatures, was all too human.

One detail which marks Linx as alien in the context of *The Time Warrior*, but not in wider society, seems to be the colour of his skin. That two prominent non-human but quasi-humanoid species have dark brown skin and are introduced in stories where all the human beings seen have white skin might well be unsettling to a white

---

[144] 'Beginning the End'.

liberal audience, even more so in 2018 than in the early 1970s. The presentation of the Ogrons as a servant species in their debut, *Day of the Daleks*, looks at best unfortunate from the second decade of the 21st century. This is not necessarily redeemed by the Doctor's description of them as mercenaries in *Frontier in Space*. Both play into western European stereotypes of black Africans, whether as enslaved labourers or the older one of the upstart ambitious outsider from renaissance drama – the best-known example being Shakespeare's Othello.[145]. The martial military commander Linx might be thought to play into a newer stereotype of the African, but one very alive in British minds in 1973, that of the dictator. The prime example of the dictator of a former British colony in 1973 was Idi Amin.

Bloodaxe describes the Doctor's 'magic' as 'black devil's work', perhaps reflecting back on Linx; but the person in the news most associated with any 'black devil' stereotype of malevolent charm and brutality was Amin[146]. His style of government was theatrical, adopting a magnified version of colonial pomp which made good television and newspaper cartoons, but the terror he practised was real. His policies most affected British lives through the expulsion of the 'Ugandan Asians', people descended from immigrants from the Indian subcontinent, planted or encouraged to settle in Uganda by Britain, first as labourers on the railway, and then to create an

---

[145] There is a vast literature on the disputed topic of the social and racial identity of African characters in renaissance drama and early modern England.

[146] Powell, Chris, 'A Phenomenological Analysis of Humour in Society' in Powell, Chris, and George EC Paton, eds, *Humour in Society: Resistance and Control*.

intermediate business class between Europeans and Africans. Amin's arguments that the Ugandan had to be supreme in his own land turned Britain's imperial assertions back against it and denied the possibility of a liberal imperialism which could be based on improving the lot of colonised peoples, as had been pleaded for in the 1940s: only the requirements of the conquerors mattered and those who had fulfilled their purpose were to be discarded. Linx does not even agree to the managed exodus of workers the Doctor suggests; his 'friends' are simply to be killed.

The British did not exist entirely in an imperial fugue in 1973. As a 1971 review of a history of British rule in Africa recognised, 'the predominant flavour of the adventure was coarse [...] national conceit, greed, snobbery' predominated[147]. Even so, the same author could find a nobility in empire which might latterly seem distasteful, especially in India. Nevertheless, in seeing how institutions inherited from the British were adapted and used by dictators such as Amin, the British audience were faced with a reflection of their own history which they were reluctant to acknowledge. Linx, with his exaggerated and sacrosanct loyalty to the Sontaran Empire justifying a string of abuses, might well have represented how the imperial officer in the field appeared to the colonised, and presented a model for emulation by those so minded.

Robert Holmes' experience of imperial warfare was in the Far East rather than in Africa. In Burma, he served in an army which fought to reverse imperial collapse and another empire's conquest. Apart from the Sontarans' similarities to the Japanese, Holmes' **Doctor Who**

---

[147] Morris, James, 'Conduct Unbecoming', *The Spectator*, 25 September 1971.

work had already featured another imperial caricature in the shape of Major Daly in *Carnival of Monsters* – depicted as a harmless buffer, but himself an exploiter of colonial labour on his way from Britain to his rubber plantation in Malaya, via the hub of British imperial domination of world trade, the Suez Canal, and ready to apply cultural stereotyping to everyone he passes. Major Daly is far closer to Linx than performance suggests and their placing in their respective plots demands; both are narrowly-focused servants of empire who take their ascendancy for granted. *Carnival of Monsters* includes the Doctor's comparison of the inhabitants of the SS *Bernice* to marine creatures transplanted from the open sea into a rock pool by a small boy[148]. The boy's viewpoint has parallels to Daly's, observing a variety of cultures under the control of, and decontextualised within, the British Empire. It also anticipates the Doctor's comparison of Linx to a boy 'stirring up the red ants and the black ants'[149]; Irongron's conflict with Sir Edward is recontextualised by Linx into a proxy war for his own entertainment and for the furthering of his imperial objective.

Perhaps the greatest influence from the former British Empire on Linx, or at least his appearance, was not from Africa or from South East Asia. Linx's earth-coloured skin tones are reminiscent of the Asaro 'mud men' masks from Papua New Guinea, from further east than Robert Holmes is known to have travelled but – as a United Nations trust territory administered by Australia from 1949 to 1975, and including territory governed in Britain's name from 1884 onwards – part of the British imperial sphere. The 'discovery' of the mud men from the 1960s onwards attracted the interests of

---

[148] *Carnival of Monsters*, Episode Three.
[149] Part Three.

photographers, documentary film-makers, and the emerging tourist industry, to the extent that establishing the origin of the mud men and their traditions is impossible to disentangle from their exploitation as a marketable symbol of the emerging state of Papua New Guinea.

The most commonly reported origin story has parallels appropriate for *The Time Warrior*: the inhabitants of the Asaro valley were defeated in warfare with their neighbours, and the survivors retreated to a muddy river bank. When the Asaro warriors moved on at nightfall, coated in mud, the victors thought they were facing the avenging spirits of the dead, and fled. This inspired the Asaro people to begin making mud masks to use in warfare; accounts then differ as to whether their conduct was mainly defensive or whether they began wars of terror and conquest on their neighbours[150]. They could be held to represent both the Doctor's improvisation and subterfuge and Linx's relentless pursuit of warfare. An alternative historical explanation emphasises the mud mask as a helmet over a bamboo and string bag frame, to facilitate vengeance assassinations rather than warfare. The custom was adapted into a dance with deliberatively stylised and sculpted masks for the Eastern Highlands Agricultural Show in 1957[151]. Far from being an expression of the survival of 'primitive' culture, it was an adapted tradition like that of the re-enactors among whom Sarah thinks she has found herself when she arrives at Irongron's castle in episode 2. There is thus some recognition of the performative in whether and how the influence of this Australasian local tradition might have shaped the appearance

---

[150] Otto, Ton, 'The Asaro Mudmen: Local Property, Public Culture?', *The Contemporary Pacific* 8/2, 1996, p353.
[151] Otto, 'The Asaro Mudmen', pp355-57.

of Linx and the ongoing iconography of the Sontarans.

Linx can thus be seen as an amalgamation of a series of very modern fears placed in medieval garb. He represents some of the uncanniness which the Doctor had once had, with extra doses of the sinister. He is the warlike part of humanity, the part which clings to claims of superiority to divide and rule. He embodies the aspects of empire which the inhabitants of the metropolitan country of an empire would rather remained abroad. Where the Daleks and the Cybermen represented fears from the atomic age, Linx incarnates a dawning historical perspective which questions Britain's role as a global power. He also casts a shadow on the assumptions behind the character of the Doctor, draws attention to the Doctor's position as assimilated immigrant, and the awkwardness of the liberal anticolonialist position the Doctor takes. The programme's inhabiting of its historical moment is further highlighted by the character of Sarah Jane Smith and the serial's attempts to develop the role of its women characters.

CHAPTER 4: 'THE WENCH IS CRAZED'

Sarah Jane Smith and Womanhood in *The Time Warrior*

> 'There were horses. It was mediaeval. There was language that isn't everyday. That helped me enormously because that gave me such a strong way of standing in a scene [...] I don't think I was ever allowed to be as strong again. I think *The Time Warrior* is the true Sarah. I loved it.'[152]

In 1984, eight years after her departure, Sarah Jane Smith was described in *Doctor Who Magazine* (DWM) as 'as much a part of the Doctor Who legend as the Time Lord himself.'[153] At Elisabeth Sladen's death in 2011, Sarah was remembered as 'iconic'[154] and 'beloved'[155]. However, in *The Time Warrior* Sarah Jane Smith is a new entity, but one who has to slip into an established position regarding the Doctor's need for a witness to his adventures, and viewers' expectations of a character who is sympathetic, likeable and attractive to enough of **Doctor Who**'s broad audience coalition.

'Am I on the Right Floor?' Being Sarah Jane Smith

Sarah Jane Smith seems to have first been conceived in terms which

---

[152] Elisabeth Sladen, in Ainsworth, John, 'Elisabeth', DWM Special Edition 23: *Sarah Jane Smith*, October 2009, p8.

[153] Marson, Richard, 'Elisabeth Sladen', DWM #89, June 1984, p24.

[154] Wicks, Kevin, 'Elisabeth Sladen, Sarah Jane from **Doctor Who**, Has Died at 63', *Anglophenia,* April 2011.

[155] Martin, Dan, 'Elisabeth Sladen Dies at 65', *The Guardian*, 20 April 2011.

are largely negative: to react against Jo Grant, characterised as dependent and 'endearingly dizzy'[156]. This reaction was presented very tentatively in what supporting media there was at the time. The unprecedentedly lengthy tenure of Barry Letts as producer and Terrance Dicks as script editor had seen the emergence of a semi-official history of **Doctor Who**, first in *The Making of Doctor Who* by Malcolm Hulke and Terrance Dicks (1972) and then in the *Radio Times* 10th Anniversary Special (1973). The special presented a core tradition of female assistants beginning with the introduction of Polly ('a weedy frightened lady') in *The War Machines* (1966) and ending with the arrival of Sarah Jane Smith in *The Time Warrior*. Sarah's qualities were presented as only a slight break from the established norm: Sarah, said Elisabeth Sladen, 'thinks she can stand on her own feet and she'll always have a bash at things believing she's right. But somebody normally ends up telling her she's totally wrong – and it's usually the Doctor'[157]. The provisional naming of the female companion (eventually Zoe) to Patrick Troughton's Doctor as 'Dolly' (for 'dolly bird') by Brian Hayles when developing a story in 1968[158], and the presumption encountered by Elisabeth Sladen from some of her male colleagues that her background must be in modelling rather than in several years of acting performance on stage and in television[159], suggest an ongoing perception that the **Doctor Who** 'assistant' was substantially a decorative cipher, not expected to be more than a teatime version of the victimised 'woman in terror' of

---

[156] Hearn, Marcus, 'The Doctor's Best Friend', DWM #440, November 2011.

[157] *Doctor Who: Radio Times Special*, 1973, reprinted 2003.

[158] Hayles, Brian, 'The Lords of the Red Planet', in Sharples, Dick, *Doctor Who: The Prison in Space*, ed Richard Bignell, p254.

[159] Sladen, Elisabeth, *The Autobiography*, p99-100.

British cinema, who while financially and often sexually liberated was otherwise unaffected by feminism[160].

Letts acknowledged that Sarah was a more assertive version of Jo Grant[161]. Jo's character arc in season 10 of **Doctor Who** had shown her taking more initiative, more successfully than in the previous two seasons, leading to her declaration of independence early in *The Green Death*. There, in short order, Jo meets and becomes engaged to Professor Cliff Jones, described to the Doctor in episode 1 as a 'sort of younger you'. Jo's future relationship with her husband is framed in terms of her rapport with the Doctor. The introduction of an independent professional young woman into the Doctor's life had the potential to reverse Jo's character arc, leaving Sarah progressively more dependent on the Doctor. This was a danger of which Terrance Dicks was aware; he later pointed to his decision to give Sarah more of the plot to shoulder in the first story of season 12, *Robot* (1974)[162]. However, as Elisabeth Sladen occasionally reflected, after *The Time Warrior*, Sarah was 'never so strong again'[163], which she recognised as a consequence of the character's need to fit into an established format.

Casting the right actor was one method of fighting against ingrained stereotypes. Letts' first choice for the role, April Walker, was chosen with contrast in mind. Her physical presence – tall, buxom, blonde –

[160] See Hutchings, Peter, '"I'm the Girl He Wants to Kill": The "Women in Peril" Thriller in 1970s British Film and Television', *Visual Culture in Britain* #10, 2009, pp53-69.

[161] 'Beginning the End'.

[162] DWM #440, November 2011.

[163] In addition to the quotation at the start of this chapter, this version appears in 'No More Sarah Jane?', DWM #163, August 1990.

allied to a varied experience as a performer (she was five years older than Katy Manning and so nearly eight years older than Manning had been when beginning work on **Doctor Who**) would have made her a more obvious counterweight to Pertwee onscreen. Pertwee and Walker had worked together before in the comedy *Oh, Clarence!* at the Lyric, London, in 1968, where Walker had played Pertwee's character's niece. Pertwee and Walker had got on well, and given Barry Letts' concern to keep his star happy following the departure of Katy Manning, it's probable that he was aware of their previous good working relationship and imagined that this would translate to **Doctor Who**. Walker was contracted on 14 March 1973. However, Pertwee soon afterwards told Letts that (in Walker's words) 'he thought I was too tall and too sexy for the part' and that viewers would think of Walker's Sarah Jane Smith as the Doctor's mistress, rather than his daughter, 'which would be totally wrong'[164]. Walker's contract was cancelled on 29 March.

Pertwee's rejection of Walker redefined the problem of replacing Katy Manning: how to find an actor who reflected Jon Pertwee's wish for someone with whom he could continue the protective relationship he'd developed for his Doctor and Jo Grant, but who was sufficiently distinct from Manning not to make the series feel as if it was treading old ground. Elisabeth Sladen was suggested to Barry Letts by Ron Craddock, producer of **Z-Cars** (1962-78). Her career was distinct from Manning's and from Pertwee's. Sladen was not from a family with theatrical or literary connections, and was from the north of England rather than the south, specifically from Liverpool where her career had begun at the Everyman Theatre. She had a history of

---

[164] Bignell, Richard 'The Original Sarah-Jane Smith', *Nothing at the End of the Lane* #3, January 2012.

television parts which reflected her north-western origins or otherwise tended towards the down-to-earth or even controversial, such as the role of student radical Sarah Collins in the **Doomwatch** (1970-72) episode *Say Knife, Fat Man* (19 June 1972) and that of thief Rose in the **Z-Cars** episode *Day Trip* (23 October 1972)[165]. While still young, she was less of an ingenue than Katy Manning might have seemed when cast in 1970, but had a breadth of experience which contrasted with Pertwee's where Walker's perhaps overlapped more. Sladen was someone to whom the comedian and variety artiste Pertwee could be seen to convey his experience within the studio confines, while onscreen Sarah Jane Smith was the new protegée of the Doctor, professionally focused on defining her situation and asking questions, but needing the Doctor's breadth of perspective.

There is very little evidence in the script of what Walker's Sarah might have been like. As Sladen remarked, Sarah Jane Smith is introduced without notes – Sladen was expected to play 'herself'. Consequently, from the start Sarah absorbs some of Sladen's personal idiom. A line in the rehearsal script for episode 1 where Sarah says the Doctor can't expect her to dance around him might have worked better with the statuesque Walker but the rehearsal script dates from a time after Sladen was cast.

There is at least one expression which appears neither in the rehearsal nor the camera scripts, Sarah Jane's 'I could just murder a cup of tea' in episode 3. If Sladen's autobiography can be relied upon, during her first year she exclaimed she could 'murder an orange'; the expression seems to be a Sladenism. The use in *The Time Warrior* is

---

[165] 'Doomwatch', 'Z Cars- Day Trip', Elisabeth Sladen website.

the earliest recorded use of 'murder' in this precise sense and manner ('To devour ravenously; to consume to the last drop or crumb') in the *Oxford English Dictionary*, albeit drawing on precedents going back to 1935[166]. Sladen deployed a precise and individual understanding of everyday idiom when playing Sarah. This also helped contrast with Katy Manning's Jo Grant whose pop culture references and slang helped define her as a reference point for a young audience juxtaposed against the military-scientific background of the Doctor and UNIT. Sarah Jane's prosaic comparisons were appropriate for the era's understanding of youth culture as a transient phase; the professional but mature Sarah Jane Smith had perhaps grown out of Jo's pop references, if she had ever used them at all. Sarah's allusions to her work and to the minutiae of living fit the recalibrated Doctor of season 11, once more journeying into space and time, and a less abrasive character than he was when Jo Grant was introduced.

Recognising that she was largely left to direct herself, Sladen wrote a list of Sarah's qualities down on part of *The Time Warrior*'s script. These are 'Righteous indignation', 'clean cut – everything obvious', 'eager for anything new', 'straight in – think later', 'impulsive'[167]. Naturally, these are all evident in the serial – her angry reaction to the Doctor's male chauvinism, her successive interpretations of Irongron's castle as village fête and full-scale re-enactment, her adopting men's clothes to raid Irongron's castle, her assumption that the Doctor must be kidnapping the scientists and helping Irongron,

---

[166] 'murder, v" (sense 9), *OED Online*. The citation is attributed 'in D.J. Howe & S.J. Walker *Doctor Who: Television Compan.* (1998) 254', the earliest printed form.
[167] 'Beginning the End'.

and her potentially suicidal attack on Linx in order to save the Doctor are a few of these features. These build on Jo Grant's comparable impulsiveness but lose her naivety and uncertainty and resignation seen in the face of some crises. They are also reminiscent of a character sidelined from the procession of former companions seen in the *Radio Times* special: Barbara Wright. Barbara was established as a mature counterpart to the schoolgirl-age character Susan and the similarly-aged Vicki; as a schoolteacher, she was the only female companion before Sarah to have a professional status and not be either a child or an 'assistant' or secretary, with the possible and qualified exception of Zoe. Sarah's directness is reminiscent of Barbara's insistence in *The Keys of Marinus* (1964) that the luxury of the city of Morphoton is a sham, or her belief that she can change the culture of the Aztecs in *The Aztecs* (1964).

The pace and structure of **Doctor Who** in 1973 was faster and much more narrowly built around the Doctor and his activities than was the series for which Barbara Wright was devised. Sarah is businesslike in her jacket and trousers, but from the beginning also girlish with an element of play. Sarah's 'Lincoln green' outfit in episodes 2 and 3 recalls a precedent which emphasises female attractiveness over practicality, a publicity still of Patricia Driscoll as Maid Marian in the TV series **The Adventures of Robin Hood**[168]. Sladen recalled that her 'boy's outfit' was 'tight'[169], although in most publicity photographs it doesn't appear so. While the camera never lingers upon her figure (unlike the dalliance with voyeurism seen in stories before and since featuring other companion characters, such

[168] Printed in *The Adventures of Robin Hood* comic vol 1 no 8, November 1957.
[169] DVD Commentary, Part Two.

as the cat-suited Zoe at the conclusion of episode 1 of *The Mind Robber* (1968), the revealingly-outfitted Leela, or Peri's bikini-clad introduction in *Planet of Fire* (1984)) the costume does emphasise the petite and unthreatening femininity Jon Pertwee sought for his co-star as well as the danger of the co-option of the pantomime 'principal boy' into Sarah's assertive character, though here the latter was avoided.

Sarah and Women's Lib

If you were a child watching **Doctor Who** in 1974, or grew up in the late 1970s and early 1980s reading **Doctor Who** books and magazines, then it's very possible that the first place you came across the term 'Women's Lib' was in connection with Sarah Jane Smith. In episode 3 of *The Monster of Peladon* (1974), the Doctor suggests she 'have a few words' with Queen Thalira, who is repressed by her male guardian and chancellor, Ortron. Sarah explains to Thalira, 'I think he was referring to Women's Lib [...] Women's liberation, your Majesty [...] it means that women don't let men push us around'. The novelisation is less subtle, with Sarah explicitly being told by the Doctor to 'Tell [Thalira] about Women's Lib!' and Sarah complying by informing the queen of Peladon that 'Women have been pushed around on Earth for a very long time, but it's all changing now'[170]. DWM informed readers in early 1981 that 'The early seventies was a period when Women's Lib was at its most vocal and so it was decided Sarah should incorporate within her personality several feminist views'[171].

---

[170] Dicks, Terrance, *Doctor Who and the Monster of Peladon*, p55.
[171] Bentham, Jeremy, 'Star Profile: Elisabeth Sladen', DWM #49, February 1981.

The introduction of a 'women's lib' companion in 1973 might seem slightly behind the times. When the first Women's Liberation Movement conference in Britain was held in 1970, the cause could still be presented in the press as an eccentric importation from the politically overwrought USA, though an alternative home-grown influence was soon recognised in the women workers' industrial action at Ford, Dagenham, in 1968, seeking equal pay[172]. The attack on the 1970 Miss World contest at the Royal Albert Hall by self-declared members of the Women's Liberation Movement (a collective of loosely affiliated regional and national organisations which began in the USA in 1967) attracted more outright hostility. One front page contrasted the victorious Jennifer Hosten (Miss Grenada) and one of the Women's Liberation Movement protesters under the headline 'The Beauty... and the Bovver Girl'[173], associating the 'women's libbers' with the 'bovver boys', skinheads provoking violence for its own sake. Perhaps because of the attack on Miss World, mainstream women politicians such as the former Labour cabinet minister Barbara Castle distanced themselves from the call for equality, declaring to the National Union of Townswomen's Guilds that, 'I want privileges for women. Men have had them for years'[174]. Sympathetic articles emphasised the 'psychological rather than political' aspect of the movement, as well as a predominant belief that 'Women's Liberation is men's liberation'[175], where more cautious ones identified the contradictions in the movement such as suspicion of already-successful women and ambiguities over support

---

[172] *The Times,* 19 October 1970; *The Observer,* 24 January 1971.
[173] *Daily Mail,* 21 November 1970.
[174] *Daily Mail,* 9 November 1970.
[175] Stott, Mary, *The Guardian,* 14 January 1971.

for corporate or state initiatives[176], or the tension between old elite 'liberated women' and the misrepresented new generation, often 'too defensive and too overworked to explain their ideas'[177].

Alongside the alarmist headlines there were concrete indications that perceptions about gender roles were being changed. The *Daily Mail* printed letters from women's liberationists eager to promote their movement – Louise Lingwood of the Women's Liberation Workshop insisted that sceptical *Mail* columnist William Davis would be greeted warmly if he came to a meeting[178]. As Robert Holmes was writing *The Time Warrior*, an article hailed 'the resurgence of drive and energy in women's organisations' in 1973, as long-established bodies such as the Townswomen's Guild and the Women's Institute formed alliances with younger more revolutionary groups around issues such as equal pay, wider issues of discrimination, and threats to child benefit[179]. Perhaps closest to **Doctor Who**'s home was the arrival of women newsreaders on BBC Radio Four in September 1972, one being Barbara Edwards, reportedly 'a leading light in the Women's Liberation Movement'[180]. This was still 'two continuity announcers out of twelve [which] still looked a rather dismal concession'[181]. Edwards became BBC Television's first woman national weather presenter on 14 January 1974, nine days after the

---

[176] Whitehorn, Katharine, 'Women's Lib: Could It Happen Here?' *The Observer*, 14 February 1971.

[177] Brittain, Victoria, 'A Conspiracy to Belittle Women's Liberation', *The Times,* 12 January 1971.

[178] *Daily Mail*, 3 April 1973.

[179] Stott, Mary, 'Action stations', *The Guardian,* 8 March 1973.

[180] *Daily Mail,* 7 September 1972.

[181] Hendy, David, *Life on Air: A History of Radio Four*, p99.

broadcast of the final part of *The Time Warrior*[182], here a single woman in a larger team of men. This was an advance on **Doctor Who**, where during her first year Elisabeth Sladen would be the only woman in an otherwise all-male established ensemble cast (in *Invasion of the Dinosaurs* and *Planet of the Spiders* (1974)); there had not been two women regulars since Jacqueline Hill's departure in 1965.

There is a precedent for Barry Letts taking up cultural movements a few years after they were seen as revolutionary. *The Dæmons* invokes the Age of Aquarius four years after the debut of the musical *Hair* which suggested that the Earth was entering a new astrological age, and flirts with New Age thinking and paganism as new things to a Saturday teatime audience (though *The Abominable Snowmen* had already explored the Buddhist side of popular New Age philosophy in 1967, at the close of the much-mythologised summer of love). Sarah's feminism probably owes more to the shift of the popular cultural centre towards equality as seen in the press, than it owes directly to anything written by either of the authors seen typically as the prophets of the Women's Liberation Movement, Betty Friedan (in *The Feminine Mystique* (1963)) or Germaine Greer (in *The Female Eunuch* (1970)). However, the realisation of Sarah as a career woman, pursuing a meaningful career in journalism, followed the advice given by Friedan to her (American) readership[183]. As one of **Doctor**

---

[182] 'Pebble Mill at One', *BBC Genome*. The news report introducing Edwards and Michael Fish as BBC weather presenters is, like Linx revealing his face at the end of *The Time Warrior*, Part One, among this author's earliest television memories.

[183] Friedan, Betty, *The Feminine Mystigue*, Chapter 14, 'A New Life Plan for Women'.

Who's asexual leads, she could not pursue the sort of revolutionary liberation proclaimed by Greer; but she could be her own person, travelling with the Doctor by choice rather than the compulsion experienced in one way or another by her predecessors.

Sarah never specifies who she works for. Her explanatory dialogue in episode 1 is minimal, only that 'all this [the concentration of scientists at the research centre, and the kidnappings] might give me a good story'. In the rehearsal script, however, she adds that she works for '*Metropolitan*', which is eventually identified onscreen as Sarah's employer in episode 1 of *Planet of the Spiders*. This sounds like a magazine due to it being a near homophone of *Cosmopolitan*, though much of *Cosmopolitan*'s content is not suitable for **Doctor Who**'s timeslot nor is Sarah's investigation in keeping with *Cosmopolitan*'s editorial policy. *Metropolitan* might also suggest one of the new generation of city magazines, led by *Time Out* in London, but again Sarah's story has little to do with entertainment listings or wider urban concerns. Perhaps all *Metropolitan* is meant to do is sound like a place 'AN ATTRACTIVE AND VITAL GIRL IN HER TWENTIES'[184] might work. Whatever it is, it has a news desk and photographers, like a Fleet Street newspaper or news agency, as Sarah wants to ring them and get a photographer sent down when she leaves the TARDIS for the first time. Confusingly, when captured and hypnotised by Linx in episode 2, the rehearsal script has Sarah reveal that she is a 'reporter for World News'. This could be a news magazine, an agency or even a television programme – as in the latter case could *Metropolitan*. In the end all was left to what Terrance Dicks termed the script's 'masterful vagueness' when

[184] As Sarah is introduced in the rehearsal and camera scripts for Part One.

discussing the story's precise historical setting[185].

Lady Eleanor

Lady Eleanor is the chatelaine of Wessex Castle and the power behind the wilting Sir Edward. She fulfils a customary role for a medieval aristocratic woman, managing her husband's resources and acting as his senior strategic adviser, planning where to send the castle's armed men or in her case, her single skilled archer, Hal.

Barry Letts regretted that Eleanor was underexplored in *The Time Warrior*. Eleanor suffers through the cuts made as rehearsal script became camera script. Onscreen, her first scene is brief: Eleanor has three speeches and Edward has two. In the rehearsal script Eleanor has eight and Edward seven, furthering Eleanor's assertiveness and Edward's dithering as well as adding extra motivation for Eleanor to seek action. She reminds Edward that Irongron's castle is his: it was lived in by Charles Audley, Edward's 'liegeman' (holding the castle as Edward's feudal vassal in return for military services) until Irongron and his robbers arrived and murdered Audley and his family. Edward's hopes for support from his neighbours are exposed as shallow: Eleanor dismisses their responses as 'Lies, evasions, excuses!'

A further scene made its way partly into the camera script; the recorded version was the last scene of the first recording day. A sequence establishing Hal and his relationship with Eleanor's servant Mary was followed by Eleanor flattering Hal's skill as an archer, the two agreeing that Eric might be captured on his way through Irongron's lands, and ending with Eleanor looking meaningfully at

---

[185] 'Beginning the End'.

Hal's bow, and Hal picking it up. The scene would have emphasised Eleanor as a manipulator and wielder of masculine power; finding her husband diminished, she sends Hal to protect the estate.

It's an irony, therefore, that it's Sarah who distracts Hal as he launches his assassination attempt. Sarah's failure to appreciate her surroundings is primarily at this point a joke on her proclaimed self-reliance and her scepticism, neither of which are serving her well. It also could be read as a comment on Sarah's individualism against the collective interest. Sarah so far has only confided to people when forced to and has kept her agenda to herself. Hal is acting because his mistress has told him this is the best way to relieve the estate from crisis. One of the strands of the story is Sarah's learning to identify the common good under the instruction of others, latterly the Doctor but firstly Lady Eleanor. It's tempting to view this as a reproof to Friedan-inspired feminism and its urging women to break out of the strictures society imposed upon them in response to the Second World War and its casting of collective security in historical male-centred terms.

Eleanor echoes Second World War arguments in the face of her husband's chivalric ethics. In another deleted scene in episode 1, Edward is 'APPALLED' at the idea he might order 'the act of a common robber! An outlaw [...] To strike a man down without warning.' His horror that Eleanor has already sent Hal to kill Irongron is placated with 'It will stop your war before it starts. It will save the lives of others, even perhaps the dear life of my own dear husband.' Barry Letts' epitome of her as a 'goody Lady Macbeth' is never more powerful than here[186]. If her husband could not screw his courage to

---

[186] DVD commentary, Part Two.

a sticking-place, then Eleanor would find someone who would.

Eleanor's name and character suggest inspiration from perhaps the most famous of all European queens in the Middle Ages, Eleanor of Aquitaine (c.1122-1204). Eleanor was the heiress of the Duchy of Aquitaine, covering most of south-west France, and the wife first of Louis VII of France and then of Henry II of England. She ruled the dynastic conglomeration of territories she and Henry had inherited jointly with him from their marriage in 1152 until 1173 when she broke with him, perhaps on an issue of dynastic policy regarding Henry's recognition of Raymond V as Count of Toulouse, a territory Eleanor claimed herself. She was imprisoned, probably in England, until Henry II died in 1189. In the last 15 years of her life she again ruled the family territories jointly with her sons Richard I (reigned 1189-1199) and John (1199-1216) until her death. As well as acting on her own account it's been suggested that many of the most astute political moves of Richard and John were those of their mother.

Eleanor of Aquitaine had featured in several Robin Hood adaptations including **The Adventures of Robin Hood**, but her most prominent realisation in 1973 was probably in the film *The Lion in Winter* (1968) based on James Goldman's play, first produced in New York in 1966. Although it does not portray a historical incident, it did introduce a cinematic audience to Eleanor, her imprisonment by her husband and their tortuous relationship with their sons. Eleanor was portrayed by Katherine Hepburn, perhaps the embodiment of mid-century Hollywood's modern independent woman. June Brown approaches Lady Eleanor as a character actor rather than as a star, and portrays this Eleanor with more decorum than Hepburn did the queen, but they have physical similarities. Brown went on to play Eleanor of Aquitaine in a provincial stage production of *The Lion in*

Winter in 1980[187].

Any association with Eleanor of Aquitaine is also a reminder of the limitations under which aristocratic women operated in medieval England. While a single woman would be regarded as a *femme sole* – legally unattached to a man – and thus would be able to govern her estates and make transactions governing land, goods and vassals on her own account, once she married, her property was regarded as her husband's for the duration of the marriage and for the husband's lifetime if they had a child, with the freedom to sell, lease, mortgage or otherwise alienate land for his lifetime or less. The lady retained a veto over a sale for more than one lifetime or in perpetuity. She had an interest in maintaining the integrity of the estate and its revenues as on her husband's death she would be entitled to a one-third interest for her own life[188]. Whatever her situation, the heiress or the married aristocratic woman was bound to the service of the fief, the feudal estate held in service from the king or sometimes an intermediate magnate. Eleanor knows how to wield power in the incapacity of her husband, but she has less freedom of action than has Sarah Jane Smith.

Mary, Eleanor's servant, is practically lost to *The Time Warrior*. In the rehearsal script, she's a strong presence in one scene in episode 1, sharing establishing dialogue with Hal before Eleanor pressures him into the assassination attempt on Irongron[189]. Like Eleanor, Mary is established to contrast with Sarah. Where Sarah is self-possessed but quick to righteous outrage, Mary is flirtatious and relaxed, happy for

---

[187] *The Stage and Television Today*, 2 January 1981.

[188] Power, Eileen, *Medieval Women*, p38.

[189] These are retained, with amendments, in the novelisation (Dicks, *The Time Warrior*, pp38-39).

Hal to distract her from preparing vegetables in the kitchen with 'A BIT OF MILD MEDIEAVAL [sic] SLAP AND TICKLE'. In what few lines she has she appears jolly and biddable where Sarah intensely seeks to lead the action. Apart from this scene, she is seen waiting on her master and mistress, their bowman and their guests Sarah and the Doctor without further development. There is some reason to think that she had a larger role in a supplanted section of episode 3.

Sarah in the Middle Ages

In the transmitted episode 3 of *The Time Warrior*, Sir Edward's premature acceptance that he will inevitably lose his castle to Irongron is followed immediately by the Doctor beginning to outline his scheme to deceive Irongron that Wessex Castle has more men to defend it than it has. In the rehearsal script there is a discussion about alternative plans. Hal still believes it's possible to mount 'a stout defence' of the castle. Edward wants to flee and steal through the forest to shelter with the Earl of Salisbury, which the Doctor thinks will only encourage Irongron to follow them. The Doctor then proposes his illusion, but Edward regrets he doesn't have more men. This is Sarah's moment. She points out that there are women in the castle too. Edward (seemingly overlooking his wife's personality) describes them as 'poor useless creatures. More mouths to feed.' Sarah insists that 'Women can fight just as well if need be'. Edward reacts as if Sarah is deluded, but Eleanor responds, 'Aye, and why not. Sooner than see Irongron take this castle, I'd don armour myself and take the field against him.' The Doctor diverts this zeal for action from the women towards his plan.

Episode 3 required the most intervention from Terrance Dicks as script editor, as Robert Holmes' proposed battle scene would have been expensive in its demands for time and a large number of supporting artists[190]. It seems possible that Sarah's plan is left over from that storyline. One might envisage Eleanor and Sarah leading a force of women, old men and children against Irongron's robbers, and the sight being so arresting that resistance is minimal (to avoid a disturbing number of onscreen deaths) and Irongron's band runs away. Perhaps Mary would have had a role in managing the women servants into a fighting force. However, there is no evidence for such a scene beyond this dead end in conversation, which arguably does not serve the women well as they accede to the Doctor's smoke bombs instead.

There are admittedly few clues which suggest that events might have taken this turn in the earlier storyline. There, Hol Mes tells Terran Cedicks that the battle for Edward's castle was inconclusive and that Linx gained the victory by setting off an explosive at a weak point in the castle walls, only for Edward and his forces to escape via a tunnel while Sarah and the Doctor dressed as mendicant friars and gained entry to Irongron's castle while he and his men were away. The Sarah figure in Holmes' storyline, 'Smith', next appears 'working with other secondaries' in the part of the castle 'where the protein requirements of the warriors were prepared'. What follows is in danger of having less to do with the conversation seen onscreen than it does with traditional battle of the sexes narratives crudely adapted to make fun of early 1970s feminism, such as *Carry On Girls* (1973), the 25th instalment in the long-running British comedy film series, then struggling to adapt to the supposedly permissive society. Sarah would exploit 'a mutually recognised hostility' between 'primaries' (men) and 'secondaries' (women) so that the women in Irongron's

---

[190] *The Complete History* #20, p101.

kitchen introduced a 'narcotic substance' into the warriors' food.

Instead, by the camera script for episode 4, Sarah has become unable to foment rebellion among the women in the kitchen. Meg's attitude has its contradictions: men are 'like children, fond of noise and brawling' but at the same time 'Women will never be free while there are men in the world, girl. We have our place'. There's an element of class, too: Irongron and his chamber guard are served stew, but the guards on the gate – 'common creatures' – and the women servants are only fed oatmeal. The rehearsal script adds some more detail: after Meg says 'But we are slaves,' she adds 'There are no freemen in all Irongron's lands'. 'Then we are slaves to slaves,' says Sarah, 'and that is worse'; but this does not shift Meg's certainty of her class and gender roles. In a small way, this is *The Time Warrior*'s equivalent of Barbara's failure to change Aztec culture in *The Aztecs*. 'History', in the guise of entrenched social attitudes, proves resistant to ideas which depend on causal chains which, from the point of view of Meg and her assistants, haven't happened yet.

The Time Warrior's evolution from storyline to camera script may well have been intended to make its representation of medieval women more authentic and its depiction of Sarah as an independent young woman less prone to parody. However, Meg's weary submission is itself an unrepresentative parody of medieval attitudes towards women. For women of Meg's class, 'rough and ready equality' was more probably the norm, as however prescribed the gender roles, men were heavily dependent on female labour[191]. Perhaps the local priest is of one of the schools of thought – again, not representative of the entire Catholic Church in the Middle Ages

---

[191] Power, *Medieval Women*, p34.

– who argued women should be subject to man, as Eve's misdemeanours had led Adam out of paradise[192]. However, as *The Time Warrior* chooses to omit almost all religious references from the broadcast version, even Irongron's remaining oath 'by the Cross' disappearing, Meg's prejudices are left without roots. The presentation of theological arguments about the relative position of the sexes would have been too nakedly controversialist for **Doctor Who**; fantastic maggots it could do as an ecological parable, but bringing Christian teaching into question would have been difficult for reasons of audience taste and the BBC's institutional position. Practicality tells over theology or even the inferred best intentions of the story, as there is no sign onscreen in episode 4 of the women in the kitchen being told to leave as Linx's take-off approaches, nor in any surviving script, nor (surprisingly for someone so attentive to retrospective editing) in Terrance Dicks' novelisation.

Sarah's suggestion that 'Women can fight just as well as men' might have horrified Sir Edward and failed to reach the camera script, but Lady Eleanor's declaration that she would armour herself and take the field against Irongron had historical precedent. Women were expected to defend their lands when their husbands were absent. The subject of women in war in medieval England was underexplored in the early 1970s, and had anyone involved with *The Time Warrior* gone looking for evidence it would have been difficult to find. Nevertheless, in the writings of earlier decades edited and collected into *Medieval Women* (1975), Eileen Power mentioned two well-remembered Scottish noblewomen who defended border castles

---

[192] Power, *Medieval Women*, p11.

against English kings[193]. One of these was in error[194], but Agnes, Countess of Dunbar, did successfully repel the siege of Dunbar Castle by the forces of Edward III in 1338[195]. Eleanor and Sarah, though, would surely have found support in the war between Empress Matilda and King Stephen for the English throne in the 1130s and 1140s, as depicted by the Flemish mercenary who wrote the *Histoire des Ducs* in the early 13th century. There, the principal strategists on both sides are women: Empress Matilda on one side and Stephen's queen, also Matilda, on the other, both of whom are more than capable of giving orders to large numbers of armed men[196].

Sarah as Gothic Heroine

If *The Time Warrior* is shaped by ideas from Gothic and Romantic literature and cinema, Sarah Jane Smith displays some characteristics of the Gothic heroine. This figure has received substantial critical examination in the decades since *The Time Warrior* was broadcast, but her outlines would have been familiar to viewers and readers as well as programme-makers. The Gothic heroine is a young woman inexperienced in the world, and of genteel if not necessarily wealthy background. She is motivated by curiosity, and often the need to right some great wrong or wrongs, to travel a distance beyond her

---

[193] Power, *Medieval Women*, p45.
[194] Although she was imprisoned at Berwick, Isabel, Countess of Buchan, had not defended its castle against Edward I in 1306 as Power thought (Watson, Fiona, 'Buchan [née Macduff], Isabel, Countess of Buchan', *Oxford Dictionary of National Biography*).
[195] Watson, Fiona, 'Dunbar, Patrick, eighth Earl of Dunbar or of March, and Earl of Moray', *Oxford Dictionary of National Biography*.
[196] Their lives would have been available to Holmes and Dicks in the *Dictionary of National Biography*.

usual experience. She is pursued by a 'man on the rampage'[197], often an older, unattractive man who desires her sexually, for her property, or both. She might seek to help or rescue an older father figure or a young man close to her own age.

Curiosity is Sarah's predominant motivating force. It's been argued that, to the male authors of 18th-century conduct books, curiosity was aimless and a 'female transgression', but for the Gothic heroine curiosity was a virtue, a means by which she crossed boundaries physical, societal and psychological to achieve 'transformation of the self'[198]. For Sarah, curiosity is a professional virtue. Although she is introduced as a young woman in a world of older men – the research centre – she functions in a society which finds a use for her curiosity, as long as she can continue to find a saleable 'story'. The young woman seeking independence merges with writer Robert Holmes' own experience as a magazine journalist and editor. This gives Sarah a transgressive focus as she crosses boundaries set by the research centre and by the Doctor (who has already rebuked Professor Rubeish for chalking an equation on the side of the TARDIS, reserving it as his space) to pursue her quest.

Sarah enters the TARDIS because she believes the Doctor might be the kidnapper of the scientists and that Professor Rubeish is being kept inside, presumably before he is smuggled out of the building. The Doctor is in Sarah's eyes the man of danger, whose plans she

---

[197] Ellis, Kate Ferguson, '"Can You Forgive Her?" The Gothic Heroine and Her Critics' in Punter, David, ed, *New Companion to the Gothic* p464.
[198] Broders, Simone, 'The Fast and the Curious: the Role of Curiosity in the Gothic Heroine's "Grand Tour of the Mind"', *English Studies* 98:8, 2017, pp917-18.

must frustrate and live to tell the tale in a magazine article. On arrival in the Middle Ages, she is almost immediately taken by force into Irongron's castle. The castle had long been allegorised as a woman, with sieges being described in male-centred terms of a righteous male lover pressing his case by force upon an unjustly unwilling female[199]. In the Gothic tradition this metaphor could be deployed in a woman's interest as an allegory of self-discovery, with both Julia in Ann Radcliffe's *A Sicilian Romance* (1790) and Emily in Radcliffe's *The Mysteries of Udolpho* (1794) exploring castles as part of their discovery of reason and their rejection of boundaries to their knowledge placed by men[200]. All Sarah wants to do is use a telephone; she already has self-knowledge, and her rough handling by Irongron's men is a crude and ultimately unsuccessful attempt to impose new boundaries on her. Later in the story, Sarah becomes adept at moving from Irongron's castle to Sir Edward's and back; her ability to operate in both spaces helps her to rescue the Doctor from death in episode 4, and is another mark of her self-possession.

Irongron has been established as a 'man on the rampage' before Sarah meets him. He is a more sensual figure than usually seen in this period of **Doctor Who**, marked onscreen by an enjoyment of food and wine which both echoes and contrasts with the more judicious appreciation shown by the Doctor in *Day of the Daleks*. His potential as a sexual threat is also marked for **Doctor Who**: he remarks that Sarah is 'not uncomely' and on Sarah's flight remarks that one of the guards will soon 'grab her tail' – which in the 14th and 15th centuries (admittedly slightly later than any date for *The Time Warrior*) could mean the lower part of the human body or

---

[199] Nicholson, 'Women on the Third Crusade', p341.
[200] Broders, 'The Fast and the Curious', pp922-23.

backside, or the genitals, especially those of a woman, and by the mid-20th century a woman as sexual object[201]. The line doesn't need to refer to the 17th-century 'taille' for a bust to have sexual connotations[202]. Irongron's views Lady Eleanor in sexual terms too, calling her a 'narrow-hipped vixen', perhaps suggesting unattractiveness and childlessness. There is no indication that Eleanor and Edward have or do not have children in the script, nor in the novelisation, but if he is alluding to the couple's lack of fertility Irongron is displaying a landholder's preoccupation with reproduction: without heirs to inherit, the lands held by Edward and Eleanor would revert to the crown and a sympathetic monarch might legitimise Irongron's claim[203]. This is not as far-fetched a situation as it might seem, as in Holmes' 'For the Attention...' storyline, Irongron is an ally of 'Kingjohn'[204]. Had Mary's very physical flirting with Hal remained, the evident vitality in the younger and socially inferior couple might have been understood as social commentary: the future of England lay in the lusty good humour of Mary and Hal, rather than in Eleanor and Edward's enervated elite, or the brutish and brutal male dominance of Irongron and his thugs.

Although there is no specific Norse figure inspiring Irongron, his name might derive in part from Old Norse 'grœnn' meaning 'green' or 'pine tree', perhaps indicating someone who despite his armour is naïve and inadequate for the task in hand. Perhaps 'Irongron' suggests 'Iron grunt', a name complementing Linx's original jargon

---

[201] 'tail, n.1.', senses 5a, 5c, 5d, *OED Online*.
[202] Cornell, Day and Topping, *The Discontinuity Guide*, p157; 'taille, n.', sense 1, *OED Online*.
[203] Power, *Medieval Women*, p39.
[204] Molesworth, *Robert Holmes*, p205.

based on American military slang. More threateningly, there might be connotations of sexual bragging: 'Iron groin'. At points in the rehearsal script Irongron is a much more frightening figure than eventually realised. His proposed 'toast to Irongron's star!' at the end of the first scene in episode 1 is followed by a closing stage direction 'MEG THE SERVING WENCH APPROACHES APPREHENSIVELY', suggesting that this is not going to be a pleasant night for her. Meg was cast and dressed in a way which plays against any tendency the script has to populate the castles with 'buxom wench' stereotypes: in the rehearsal script she is 'A PLUMP, NOT UNATTRACTIVE SERVING GIRL WHO HAS SEEN BETTER DAYS', but in casting and dressing Sheila Fay the decision was made to emphasise hard work, a poor diet and the rigours of medieval existence.

The Gothic heroine is always in danger of becoming a victim. Walpole in *The Castle of Otranto* placed Isabella under threat of forced marriage and rape, while her would-be violator Manfred killed his own daughter, Matilda. Some authors in the heyday of the Gothic novel enjoyed subverting the expectations of an audience bred up on the writings of Radcliffe. Matthew Lewis' *The Monk* (1796) with its 'emphatic masculine ambience' dwells on its eponymous character Ambrosio's rape and murder of his long-lost sister Antonia[205]. For the anticlerical Lewis, it's the confinement of Ambrosio's 'warrior spirit' in the role of a monk which lead him to moral degradation. Irongron and Linx are both warriors and have no problems with moral degradation despite not having the benefit of clergy. Linx is the more interesting parallel as he is removed from sexual identity – the ideal of a tonsured monk – but is only a frustrated warrior because chance has cut him off from the war he

---

[205] Smith, Andrew, *Gothic Literature*, p29.

was fighting. If anyone in *The Time Warrior* violates Sarah, it is Linx. Where Irongron only touched Sarah to take her necklace from her (a change from the rehearsal script's watch, both less complicated in terms of camera shots and avoiding exposing Irongron to 20th-century technology for which Sarah was responsible), Linx strokes Sarah's neck as part of his examination of her 'thorax [...] of a different construction'. Linx then uses his all-purpose weapon-wand to force Sarah to surrender information about her identity and origins and obscure her memory of encountering him.

Nevertheless, Sarah is not laid low, but almost immediately helps Hal's escape from the castle. Sarah's refusal to be cowed by repeated hypnotisms and possessions of other kinds becomes perhaps her defining characteristic. The ability of the enemy to copy or subsume Sarah – as in *The Android Invasion* (1975) and *The Masque of Mandragora* (1976) – communicates to the audience how serious a threat they are. It could be argued that Sarah's self-knowledge is part of her appeal – Elisabeth Sladen's note that everything to Sarah is absolutely concrete in a given situation – and throughout the character's time in **Doctor Who** successive antagonists try to take that from her. They fail; although the Doctor's role in 'restoring' her to herself gradually increases, complementing Sladen's observation that Sarah's outfit in her final story, *The Hand of Fear* (1976), shows her 'so far removed from reality now that it was time for her to go'[206]. Perhaps, then, it is the least aggressive of the men on the rampage who is the most dangerous.

In the context of the stories preceding *The Time Warrior*, Sarah's succumbing to Linx's control illustrates one of the ways in which she

---

[206] *The Hand of Fear*, Part One, DVD commentary track.

is a different kind of heroine to Jo. In *Frontier in Space*, Jo successfully resists being hypnotised by the Master, using a method which she specifically says the Doctor taught her. The exercise is reminiscent of the mental arithmetic the Doctor practices with Jo to enable them to resist the influence of the 'brainstorm' suffered by Axos in *The Claws of Axos* and the incident recalls Jo being placed under the Master's influence in *Terror of the Autons*. Arguably, the Doctor's 'deprogramming' of Jo in episode 2 of *Terror of the Autons* is the first time he accepts responsibility for her. Sarah's shaking off Linx's influence herself is to some extent a contrast with Jo, though Linx's ambitions are different too: he wants information, while the Master wanted to use Jo as a weapon. Nevertheless, in this story Sarah is not a vessel for anybody.

Comparably, Sarah also avoids the romantic – perhaps Romantic-Gothic – plots which were established for Jo. Jo has a list of suitors and would-be father-figures, where in this season Sarah's relationships with men are friendly but there is no-one making direct romantic overtures. In contrast, Jo's confirmation to the Doctor that she wants to travel with Professor Jones 'more than anything else in the world' towards the end of *The Green Death* is almost an exact quotation from the 1938 *Adventures of Robin Hood*, spoken by Olivia de Havilland's Marian on confirming she wants to marry Robin. On one hand Jo drew from an archetype of the fairytale heroine, the orphan (a dependent of 'relatives in high places' in *Terror of the Autons*, specifically of an uncle by *Frontier in Space*) looking for people to support and be supported by, leading to a series of handsome princes seeking her hand – a Snow White, with the Doctor and the men of UNIT as her dwarfs. Jo travelled into the forest of adventure and found knowledge; she rejects wealth, power and the future for love and adventure and present-day Earth. In contrast, Sarah's adventures lack this arc; her curiosity is both professional and personal and gets her into trouble on her own accord.

Sarah and the Doctor

In episode 4, Linx describes Sarah as the Doctor's 'female companion'. This might jar slightly for some of the audience. Sarah did not arrive in medieval England as the Doctor's travelling companion. She isn't even his 'assistant' in the tradition established in the UNIT era by which Liz Shaw and Jo Grant are both appointed as aides to the Doctor. When precisely do Sarah and the Doctor throw in their lots with each other, and what might this say about them?

Sarah and the Doctor don't become allies until the second half of the story. The Doctor seems to regard her as a potential friend from the beginning, but Sarah treats his chatter as obfuscation – 'Kindly don't be so patronising' – and she believes that the Doctor is the kidnapper as late as episode 3. Her continued focus on the missing scientists leads her to demote the mystery of the TARDIS to a secondary priority and she is caught off-guard when the Doctor raises it. Elisabeth Sladen chooses to change Sarah's demeanour from assertive confidence to confusion when the Doctor reveals he works for UNIT, after which the two don't really get to know each other until the scene in Sir Edward's Tower Room, where Sarah finds the Doctor mixing his 'singularly noxious compound' and chastises him for getting women to do all the dirty work while men have all the fun.

'Fun' is a key word. The Doctor takes the businesslike Sarah and teaches her how to play. She's already enjoyed being Sir Edward's art teacher and arrives brandishing one of the dummies' faces on a stick.

He enjoys teasing her – 'I'm glad I decided to let you stay,' he says, though it's not obvious how he would have excluded her from the action. The Doctor's sense of fun is bound up with his moral code: he enjoys helping Sir Edward, but does so because he has a job to do involving 'the whole future of your species'. The Doctor's explanation of the Time Lords undermines the potential for pomposity in the scene and parries Sarah's directness. Sarah subsequently reveals the remaining gulf between her and the Doctor when she suggests that he's inflicted 'some kind of (poison) gas' on Irongron and his men. The Doctor is appalled; but there is a parallel with Lady Eleanor, who assumes that the 'little draught' the Doctor proposes to mix is 'a magic potion' to kill Irongron. Human beings fear and plan the worst, but the Doctor attempts to take a route which will cause the least harm and entertain himself while pursuing it.

The redefinition of the Time Lords as 'galactic ticket inspectors' deromanticises the moment and the Doctor. If Sarah is considered a Gothic heroine, this is something of a *Northanger Abbey* moment, in that Jane Austen's Catherine Morland learns through experience the reality of a world of great houses and old families which she had understood previously through the fantasies of Gothic fiction. A human of secret power becomes a traffic warden from space – the unfathomable becomes the absurd.

Between the rehearsal and the camera scripts, the Tower Room scene lost several minutes of dialogue. This would have revealed that the Doctor was battling for the existence of Sarah's world – if Linx succeeded in arming Irongron with rifles and robots, Sarah's 20th century would never happen at all. This excision obscured the running concern with changing history through this story and its successor, *Invasion of the Dinosaurs*. Sarah's future is under threat, as Holmes would emphasise further in his later serial, *Pyramids of Mars* (1975)[207]; but understatement was perhaps advisable here given the demands the serial was already placing on the audience and the dangers of including too similar a threat to that in the imminent *Invasion of the Dinosaurs*.

The final scene of episode 3 casts Sarah in a role previously associated with Jo Grant and several of her predecessors, the voice of compassion for individuals when the Doctor can only see the larger picture. In this case she wants to feed the kidnapped scientists who are collapsing from near starvation, but the Doctor is concentrating on the imminent departure of Linx and the possibility that Irongron will survive armed with Linx's weaponry. The Doctor confirms his reliance on Sarah when Professor Rubeish questions her presence and assumes she is implicated. This leads into episode 4, which begins with Sarah's deflection of Linx's 'ray tube' from the Doctor, and during which Linx identifies her as the Doctor's 'female companion' shortly before attempting to kill her. The subsequent restraint of Linx, stunned by a blow to the probic vent, leads to this exchange, as Sarah goes to drug the food being prepared for Irongron and his men:

DOCTOR

You'll be careful?

[SARAH NODS]

---

[207] Credited to 'Stephen Harris' but written by Holmes after he took over a story which as script editor he had originally commissioned from Lewis Greifer.

SARAH

You too, Doctor.

The non-verbal element recalls Katy Manning's Jo Grant's rapport with Pertwee's Doctor, and helps overcome any lingering audience resistance.

Sarah and the Doctor are reunited when she effects the Doctor's escape from Irongron's men by swinging an opportunely-placed chandelier across the Great Hall in his direction, so he can leave through the door. The Doctor thanks her, and calls her Sarah, whereas in the camera script he still reverts to 'Miss Smith' at this point; Pertwee presumably followed his instincts concerning the relationship between the two. There's more than a touch of self-congratulation in the line, as if the Doctor is more grateful for Sarah providing him with the opportunity to pose as 'the daring young man on the flying trapeze' than saving his life as such. This both underlines the Doctor's unflappability and his sense of humour, and Sarah's increasing grasp of his mode of action. She again echoes Jo in insisting that she accompanies the Doctor back to Irongron's castle to finish the rescue of the prisoners, though once there she has little to do other than join Rubeish in sending the scientists back to the research centre. When Sarah takes charge and despatches Rubeish to the 20th century, her decision dispels any lingering doubt that Sarah has committed to seeing the adventure through and incorporates her into the Doctor's ongoing travels. 'Companionisation' passes a crucial stage.

Sarah rescues the Doctor again by reviving him after he was rendered near-unconscious in his fight with Linx. There are echoes of the Gothic here too, as Sarah's self-possession intervenes to change the outcome of a wrestling match which is reminiscent of a drawing by Fuseli[208] as well as the clash between the Doctor and the physical representation of the 'dark side' of Omega's mind in *The Three Doctors*. In turn the dark side of Omega's mind bears some relation to William Blake's 'Ghost of a Flea' (c1819-20). The Gothic imagery evoked biblical precedent too, that of Jacob wrestling with God. Sarah's intervention is at least tentatively readable as a mortal daring to challenge one godlike as they passed judgement on another – an understated variant of the climax of *The Dæmons*.

After this, the Doctor is in Sarah's charge and she pokes respectful fun as they depart, which again recalls *The Dæmons* in which the Doctor denies that he is a magician after performing feats based on advanced scientific knowledge which might as well be magic. Audience familiarity has been established so that Sarah can be slotted in to the UNIT framework with little difficulty in *Invasion of the Dinosaurs*, while retaining the advantage of a questioning and little-monitored outsider.

It's proved difficult to discuss Sarah's relationship with the Doctor solely in terms of their characters. The needs of the programme's format, particularly the provision of a new female companion figure to replace Jo Grant, are always apparent. This is something a much later version of **Doctor Who** would foreground, with stylised 'Doctor Who?' or 'Doctor What?' scenes introducing Clara (in *The Snowmen* (2012)) and Bill (in *The Pilot* (2017)). The lingering impression, though, is of Sarah's curiosity and impetuousness being presented as a professional and personal drive rather than Jo's combination of

---

[208] Fuseli, Henry, attrib, 'Wrestlers'. 18th or early 19th century. British Museum, *Artstor*.

childlike enthusiasm and a need to support and be supported. The Doctor's explanation of the Time Lords as 'galactic ticket inspectors', however flippant, appeals to Sarah's sense of identity as a reporter. It's their shared quasi-professional interest in investigation and righting wrongs that binds the two.

> 'Sarah Jane Smith was created to bring the illusion of equality to the series, and to a large extent she succeeded [...] It is sad that she is constantly forced either to follow the Doctor blindly or strike out on her own, only to have to be rescued.'[209]

It is questionable whether any character in **Doctor Who** can be the Doctor's equal. Even those with comparable or apparently greater power must be exposed as possessing ultimately fatal weakness – a recurrent example being the Master – or be outwitted through their Olympian position blinkering them to the Doctor's guile, such as the Toymaker in *The Celestial Toymaker* (1966). In terms of gender equality, **Doctor Who** had sometimes exploited differences in gender roles to resolve plots or aspects of them – whether the crucial roles Polly's coffee-making and nail varnish remover perform in the defeat of the Cybermen in *The Moonbase* (1967), or the screams of Victoria directed against the weed creatures in *Fury from the Deep*. The attributes of girlhood or womanhood could be shown to have power over the monsters of **Doctor Who** as much as the Doctor's masculine knowledge or the fighting skills of a Chesterton, a McCrimmon or a Lethbridge-Stewart. However, Sarah had the most gender-neutral career identity given to a companion since Barbara Wright. Her outfit and demeanour are businesslike, which distance her from the more conventionally (if occasionally striving for the futuristic) feminine

---

[209] Stirling, Helen, 'Girl Talk', *In-Vision* 17: *Sarah Special,* June 1989.

attire of her predecessor as a professional accompanying the Doctor, Liz Shaw. Instead, the gap between Sarah and the Doctor is not one primarily of age and gender but of experience and perspective. Where Sarah adopts a conventional feminine role, in the kitchen scenes, she seems just as performative as she does in her 'boy's clothes'. For Sarah, women's servitude in the kitchen is historical. That it was not in the lived or observed experience of the audience helped the 10-year-old **Doctor Who**'s claim to continued modernity and a progressive outlook. Whatever would happen to Sarah Jane Smith in her future, here her association with the Doctor is shown as one of choice, and she does the rescuing. Even if total equality between the leads in **Doctor Who** was elusive, the steps made to enhance Sarah's credibility and agency were not illusory as far as *The Time Warrior* was concerned.

CONCLUSION: THE SONTARAN INHERITANCE

The Time Warrior and Doctor Who

Made as part of the 1972-73 production block, but always intended to be transmitted as the opening serial in the 1973-74 season, *The Time Warrior* projected the concerns of the end of season 10 into season 11. Its role in reinforcing Barry Letts' authorial signature as a producer is neglected. Letts fuelled the adventure stories of **Doctor Who** by building stories around his own apprehensions about human beings' (at best) neglect of or (at worst) malign intent towards their environment. Stories inspired by contemporary anxieties about technology were an established part of **Doctor Who** from *The Daleks* (1963-64), but Letts (with Terrance Dicks) brought a more systematic approach to tales of apocalypses imminent or historic, commissioning serials which extended the old themes of new technology running amok but dwelling with more consistency on the implications for living things and their environment, with an added consideration of individual and collective responsibility.

The Time Warrior is one of a sequence of stories which balance situations pessimistic about the direction of change with hope that a good future can be found for humanity. *The Green Death* takes human desire for profit and order above all else – expressed through corporate greed and mechanisation – and presents it as maggot-inviting decay, with the co-operative living and sustainable eco-science of Professor Jones and the Nuthutch residents proving the salvation the Doctor and UNIT are looking for. Where *The Green Death* was about forces in the present competing over the future, *The Time Warrior* is a story of someone in the past – Linx – wanting to change the present (as lived in by the audience) to suit their own narrow aims, and encouraging the worst of humanity as he does so. The fears of both *The Green Death* and *The Time Warrior* are restated in the narrations read by Butler (Martin Jarvis) in the reminder room scenes in *Invasion of the Dinosaurs*. There, rough analogues of Sir Edward, Linx and Irongron – Sir Charles Grover, Professor Whitaker and General Finch – present a more powerful representation of the establishment than met in either of the preceding stories. These three are united in wanting not just to change the future and the present, but to erase most of the human past as well, in the hope of guiding humanity not to repeat its mistakes. The sequence ends with *Death to the Daleks* (1974), where the Doctor and Sarah fight the Daleks against the background of a society whose reliance on technology has led to its fall and the perpetuation of Exxilon as an inhospitable world which serves the polluting city rather than living organic beings. Even then, it is not too late to break the cycle of desolation if a concerted effort can be made. In every case, key figures are shirking or have avoided their responsibilities. The pursuit of narrow self-interest coincides with attempts to reshape complex presents into simpler forms. Linx denies his responsibility towards his fellow life-forms as much as Whitaker, Grover, and Finch deny their responsibility towards all but a chosen few.

Several of the concerns of *The Time Warrior* recur in Robert Holmes' later scripts for **Doctor Who**. In *The Time Warrior*, the Doctor warns of what Linx's actions will do to humanity's future, but *Pyramids of Mars* makes the threat to the audience's (and Sarah's) present concrete by taking Sarah to a '1980' devastated by the Osiran Sutekh, who exists only to destroy. Sutekh is godlike, but Linx is not the only deluded empire-builder visiting Earth's past with the intent of reclaiming their future. Magnus Greel's interference in the 19th century in Holmes' *The Talons of Weng-Chiang* seems to have minimal damage to Earth's future. It's logical that Greel would want to be as unobtrusive as possible, for he wants to return to the 51st century much as Linx wants to return to his space war in the 13th.

Among other stories commissioned by Holmes when script editor, *The Masque of Mandragora* by Louis Marks includes another extraterrestrial force, the Mandragora Helix, seeking to change the future by destroying the foundation for humanity's technological progress, and thus encourage the superstition on which it feeds. *The Hand of Fear* by Bob Baker and Dave Martin (but with substantial input from Holmes as an ambitious six-parter was restructured into a manageable four-episode story) went further in introducing Eldrad, who eventually proposes the recreation of his dictatorship, which destroyed his own world of Kastria in the remote past, on Earth. All these stories emphasise the vulnerability of causality and question the inevitability of Sarah's (and the audience's) present day or indeed the prospect of a spacefaring technological humanity as seen in **Doctor Who**'s future-set stories.

As *The Time Warrior* amplifies Holmes' concerns with imperial activity in Asia, already present in *Carnival of Monsters*, so it points towards subsequent empire-themed Holmes *Doctor Who* tales. *The Ark in Space* (1975) at first shows the triumph of an 'indomitable' humanity, cryogenically preserved on Space Station Nerva, 'out amongst the stars […] ready to outsit eternity,' in the Doctor's famous speech in episode 1. The Wirrn, who have infiltrated the space station and assimilated the knowledge and bodies of humans, believe they have justice on their side, having been forced from their 'old lands' in Andromeda by human colonists. While 'a vestige of the human spirit' wins the day when the human leader Noah, transformed into a Wirrn, leads the other members of his new species to their destruction in episode 4, the moral superiority of that spirit has been questioned, much as revelations of atrocities in Vietnam undermined the assumption of moral supremacy by American and European culture. References to the Filipino advance on Reykjavik in *The Talons of Weng-Chiang* are slender, but might suggest an oriental vengeance on the West which Holmes might easily find justified. His first villain in *Talons*, Li H'sen Chang, is himself potentially viewable as a colonised person. Like Irongron wielding modern weapons and Noah changed mind and body into a Wirrn, he has become the instrument of Magnus Greel, who has distorted Chang's culture to serve his own ends.

A more explicit parallel appears in *The Sun Makers* (1977), where the Company is both the (Usurian) commercial exploiter of the human colony on Pluto and a tax-collecting state. This duality recalls the East India Company, which had a monopoly of British commerce with India from 1600. From the mid-18th century it assumed more and more of the characteristics of a state, the British Crown only asserting its superiority over the Company's territories in India in stages between 1784 and 1858, finally dissolving it in 1874. As in India, the colonisers delegate much administration to the colonised. The Collector's dismissal of the Time Lords in episode 3, that Gallifrey 'was classified grade three in the last market survey, its potential for market development being correspondingly low' recalls Linx's poor opinion of the Time Lords' ability to resist a determined assault. Trade and conquest were the two arms of the East India Company and the European empires in Asia, but Sontaran and Usurian alike express the complacency of established authority in the face of a threat they don't believe, suggesting both the 18th-century Mughal Empire's belief that the gains of a power as seemingly disunited as the East India Company must be inevitably limited, and the underappreciation of Japan's military capabilities by the British administrations in Burma and Malaya in 1941-42. The curious naming of the gun-runner Rohm-Dutt in *The Power of Kroll* (1978) after the Indian administrator, literary scholar and economic historian Romesh Chunder Dutt (1848-1909), deserves exploration beyond the context of this chapter[210].

Even Irongron and his company have their successors. Although they become the Doctor's allies rather than his enemies, the Others led by Mandrel in *The Sun Makers* have filth and brutality and cynicism in common with Irongron and his men; their redemption comes from the Doctor and Leela showing them that they can have greater ambitions than mere survival, where Linx only offers Irongron the possibility that he can be king rather than just a legitimated landholder (as would seem to be his ambition, implicitly, in the original storyline).

John Friedlander's Sontaran mask had a pedigree in the late-18th and early 19th-century Gothic. As a child I regarded the Sontarans as no laughing matter. Their faces were distortions of human features, shrunken and squashed in huge heads. Nevertheless, there was more humour in the creatures than I recognised at the time, particularly in Linx, at narrowest a parody of an officer in the colonies unable and unwilling to appreciate his host environment on its own terms, whose appearance was remembered by its designer as a

---

[210] Raychaudhuri, T, 'Dutt, Romesh Chunder [Rameshchandra Datta] (1848–1909), Administrator in India and Author', *Oxford Dictionary of National Biography*.

visual gag. It's a gag which impressed itself on Nancy Banks-Smith, who greeted Linx as the Doctor's 'new buddy for all the world like a baked potato.'[211] The image of the Sontaran as potato spread in homes and playgrounds, and for a lot of the audience they must have been a thoroughly domesticated menace. The frustration of some modern commentators with the presentation of the Sontarans – especially Strax, introduced in *A Good Man Goes to War* (2011) and increasingly overtly comedic – is arguably in defiance both of widespread public reception of the aliens and of authorial intention.

'But do you know the time?'[212]

The Time Warrior found a way in which **Doctor Who** could once more visit human history, enhancing the time travel aspect of its format while avoiding the didacticism recalled from the 1960s historicals. Its blend of a threatened present and pastiche of established depictions of history in fiction set the tone for the next decade of **Doctor Who**'s excursions into the past. *Pyramids of Mars* and *The Talons of Weng-Chiang* both exploited established fictional milieus but said less than *The Time Warrior* about the periods they visited. In its general introduction to themes surrounding a period, *The Masque of Mandragora* is a closer match in its borrowings from Renaissance drama, while *Horror of Fang Rock* (1977) relies on the humans threatened by the alien being distracted by the difficulties of managing technological change in the lighthouse. The problem of pastiche is that it could displace other elements: *The Androids of Tara* (1978) annoyed some commentators by being too straightforward a borrowing from Anthony Hope's novel *The Prisoner*

---

[211] *The Guardian*, 17 December 1973, p8.
[212] The Doctor to Rubeish, Part Two.

of Zenda (1894) and its cinematic adaptations, where *Black Orchid* (1982) copied the atmosphere and trappings of a 1920s murder mystery without offering any examination of the period nor including a science-fiction element other than the TARDIS. *The Visitation* (1982), with its stranded Terileptils in 1660s London and playfulness with historical details, owed more to *The Time Warrior.* Probably *The Mark of the Rani* (1985), with its concentrated attempt to bring in several historical figures, decisively broke with *The Time Warrior*'s model, with later stories choosing to deal in specifics of time and historical personality eschewed by the broad brushes of Robert Holmes.

The Time Warrior remains a story rooted in post-war, post-imperial Britain. It is interested in telling an adventure story first and foremost, but the parallels with which the script entertains itself, and sections of the audience, are the building blocks for that adventure and its resolution inevitably suggests an answer for the problems of the day on which it plays, however impartial or simplistic. The Doctor and the programme stand not only for rational enquiry, but for compassion as a feature of the rational mind. Cruelty spirals onwards unless stopped, and it is the ordinary human being who has the power to end the cycle of indiscriminate violence even if that includes the targeted use of the methods of war themselves. The lesson of empire is that imperialism must be renounced and replaced with internationalism and inter-speciesism. Even if this is something that the real-life descendants of the fictional Hal and Mary had still to learn in 1974, one still taught the children in hope. After all, of the two spacemen seen in armour in *The Time Warrior*, it's the Doctor who most resembles the suit of armour on the *John Bull* cover, and who represents the kind of childhood hopes this era of **Doctor Who** wishes fulfilled in adult life.

ACKNOWLEDGEMENTS

The composition of this book has been helped by several people. An encouraging conversation in 2016 with James Brough, Penny Goodman and Holly Matthies sharpened my ideas and enthusiasm, and Ian Potter reintroducing me to James Cooray Smith at the BFI's Missing Believed Wiped later that year led to the invitation to write for **The Black Archive**.

As usual on my ventures into the production history of **Doctor Who**, the BBC Written Archives Centre was immensely helpful. My thanks also to the anonymous collector who allowed me access to their copies of the rehearsal scripts for *The Time Warrior*, which changed the direction of this book for the better.

Others whose assistance, feedback, ideas and suggestions informed my writing include Alan Stevens, Andrew O'Day, Andrew Pixley, Erin Horáková, Fiona Moore, Ian Bayley, Katrin Thier, Melissa Beattie, Richard Molesworth, Stephen Brennan-Bell and William Shaw. Grounding conversation came in particular from Paul and Sheena Dumont, while Una McCormack was greatly supportive as the prolonged business of completing a first draft neared its end.

Paul Simpson has been immeasurably patient waiting for my manuscript and I'm grateful to him, Philip Purser-Hallard and Stuart Douglas for resolving problems and seeing this book through to publication.

Bibliography

Documents

BBC Written Archives Centre.

> **Doctor Who** General File, 'A', T5/647/1.

> **Doctor Who** Serial UUU, *The Time Warrior*, T5/2559/1.

> **Doctor Who** Series UUU scripts, *The Time Warrior*, TS2/69/1 (camera scripts).

Private collection.

> **Doctor Who**, *The Time Warrior* (rehearsal scripts).

Books

Allen, Louis, *Burma: The Longest War 1941-45*. London, Phoenix, 2000. ISBN 9780304353705.

Allibone, Jill, *Anthony Salvin*. Cambridge, Lutterworth Press, 1987. ISBN 9780718827076.

Baker, Bob, *K-9 Stole My Trousers*. UK, Fantom Publishing, 2013. ISBN 9781781961322.

Barczewski, Stephanie L, *Myth and National Identity in Nineteenth-Century Britain*. Oxford, Oxford University Press, 2000. ISBN 9780198207283.

Bennett, Alan, Peter Cook, Jonathan Miller and Dudley Moore, *The Complete Beyond the Fringe*. London, Methuen, 2003. ISBN 9780413773685.

Bentham, Jeremy, *The Companion Volume*. London, Doctor Who

Appreciation Society, 1977.

Britton, Piers D, and Simon J Barker, *Reading Between Designs: Visual Imagery and the Generation of Meaning in The Avengers, The Prisoner* and *Doctor Who.* Austin, TX, University of Texas Press, 2003. ISBN 9780292709270.

Butler, David, ed, *Time And Relative Dissertations In Space.* Manchester, Manchester University Press, 2007. ISBN 9780719076824.

> Charles, Alec, 'The ideology of anachronism'.
>
> O'Mahony, Daniel, '"Now how is that wolf able to impersonate a grandmother?" History, pseudo-history and genre in **Doctor Who**'.

Calvert, Michael, *Fighting Mad.* London, Jarrolds, 1964.

Chapman, FS, *The Jungle is Neutral.* London, Chatto and Windus, 1949.

Clausewitz, *On War (Vom Kriege).* 1832. A Rapoport, ed, London, Penguin, 1968. ISBN 9780140444278.

Cornell, Paul, Martin Day, and Keith Topping, *Doctor Who: The Discontinuity Guide.* London, Virgin Publishing, 1995. ISBN 9780426204428.

Cox, Howard, and Simon Mowatt, *Revolutions from Grub Street: A History of Magazine Publishing in Britain.* Oxford, Oxford University Press, 2013. ISBN 9780199601639.

Dicks, Terrance, *Doctor Who and the Invasion of Time.* **The Target Doctor Who Library** #35. London, WH Allen, 1980. ISBN 9780426200932.

Dicks, Terrance, *Doctor Who and the Monster of Peladon.* **The Target Doctor Who Library** #43. London, WH Allen, 1980. ISBN 9780426201328.

Dicks, Terrance, *Doctor Who and the Time Warrior.* **The Target Doctor Who Library** #65. London, WH Allen, 1978. ISBN 9780426200239.

Friedan, Betty, *The Feminine Mystigue*, new edition. New York, WW Norton, 2013. ISBN 9780393346787.

Gerrard, Christine, *The Patriot Opposition to Walpole: Politics, Poetry and National Myth 1725-1742.* Oxford, Oxford University Press, 1994. ISBN 9780198129820.

Gibson, James William, *The Perfect War: Technowar in Vietnam.* Boston and New York, Atlantic Monthly Press, 1986. ISBN 9780871130631.

Groom, Nick, *The Gothic: A Very Short Introduction.* Oxford, Oxford University Press, 2017. ISBN 9780199586790.

Hendy, David, *Life on Air: A History of Radio Four.* Oxford, Oxford University Press, 2007. ISBN 9780199248810.

Howard, Anthony, *RAB: The Life of RA Butler.* London, Jonathan Cape, 1987. ISBN 9780224018623.

Howe, David J, Mark Stammers, and Stephen James Walker, *Doctor Who: The Handbook – The First Doctor.* London, Virgin Publishing, 1994. ISBN 9780426204305.

Hulke, Malcolm and Dicks, Terrance, *The Making of Doctor Who.* London, Pan Books. 1972. ISBN 9780330232036.

Lofficier, Jean-Marc, *The Doctor Who Programme Guide* Volume 2. London, W.H. Allen. 1981. ISBN 9780491028851.

Lofficier, Jean-Marc, *Doctor Who: The Terrestrial Index*. London, Virgin Publishing. 1991. ISBN 9780426203612.

Lupack, Alan, *The Oxford Guide to Arthurian Literature and Legend*. Oxford, Oxford University Press. 2005. ISBN 9780192802873.

Marson, Richard, *Blue Peter: Inside the Archives*. 2nd edition. Dudley, Kaleidoscope. 2010. ISBN 9781900203302.

Marter, Ian, *Doctor Who and the Sontaran Experiment.* **The Target Doctor Who Library** #56. London: W.H. Allen. 1978. ISBN 9780426200499.

Mason, EC, *The Mind of Henry Fuseli*. London, Routledge and Kegan Paul, 1951. ASIN B0000CHWF5.

Miller, Keith, *The Official Doctor Who Fan Club* vol 1: *The Jon Pertwee Years*. Edinburgh, Pegimount, 2012. ISBN 9780957370401.

Molesworth, Richard, *Robert Holmes: A Life in Words*. Prestatyn, Telos, 2013. ISBN 9781845830915.

Mutsu, Hirokichi, ed, *The British Press and the Japan-British Exhibition of 1910*. Melbourne, Melbourne Institute of Asian Languages and Societies, 2001. ISBN 9780734021038.

Myles, LM, *The Ambassadors of Death.* **The Black Archive** #3. Edinburgh, Obverse Books, 2016. ISBN 9781909031395.

Orthia, Lindy, ed, *Doctor Who and Race*. Bristol, Intellect, 2013. ISBN 9781783200368.

> Orthia, Lindy A, 'Savages, Science, Stagism, and the Naturalized Ascendancy of the Not-We in **Doctor Who**'.

Parkin, Lance, and Lars Pearson, *Ahistory: An Unauthorized History of the Doctor Who Universe*, 3rd edition. Des Moines, IA, Mad Norwegian Press, 2012. ISBN 9781935234111.

Powell, Chris, and George EC Paton, eds, *Humour in Society: Resistance and Control.* Basingstoke, Macmillan, 1988. ISBN 9780333440711.

> Powell, Chris, 'A Phenomenological Analysis of Humour in Society'.

Postles, Dave, *Naming the People of England, c1100-1350.* Newcastle upon Tyne, Cambridge Scholars Publishing, 2006. ISBN 9781904303879.

Potter, Ian, *Carnival of Monsters.* **The Black Archive** #16. Edinburgh, Obverse Books,. 2018. ISBN 9781909031623.

Power, Eileen, *Medieval Women.* Cambridge, Cambridge University Press, 1975. ISBN 9780521099462.

Preddle, Jon, *Timelink.* 2nd edition, volume 2. Prestatyn, Telos, 2011. ISBN 9781845830052.

Punter, David, *A New Companion to the Gothic.* 2nd edition. Chichester, Wiley-Blackwell. 2012, ISBN 9781405198066.

> Ellis, Kate Ferguson, '"Can You Forgive Her?" The Gothic Heroine and Her Critics.'

Richards, Jeffrey, *Swordsmen of the Screen: From Douglas Fairbanks to Michael York.* London, Routledge and Kegan Paul, 1977. ISBN 9780710084781.

Scott, Walter, *Ivanhoe.* 1820. Graham Tulloch, ed, Edinburgh, Edinburgh University Press, 1998. ISBN 9780748605736.

Scott, Walter, *Minstrelsy of the Scottish Border*. 2nd edition, volume 1. Edinburgh, Ballantyne for Longman and Rees, Manners and Miller, and A Constable, 1803.

Seeley, JC *The Expansion of England*. London, Macmillan, 1883.

Sendall, Bernard, *Origin and Foundation, 1946–62*. **Independent Television in Britain** volume 1. Basingstoke, Macmillan, 1982. ISBN 9780333539286.

Sharples, Dick, *Doctor Who: The Prison in Space*. Richard Bignell, ed, Kent, Nothing at the End of the Lane, 2011. ASIN B009ANL962.

Shelley, Mary, *Frankenstein, or the Modern Prometheus*. 1818 revised 1831. 1818 text ed Nick Groom, Oxford, Oxford University Press. 2018, ISBN 9780198814047.

Sladen, Elisabeth, *The Autobiography*. London, Aurum, 2011. ISBN 9781845134884.

Smith, Andrew, *Gothic Literature*. Edinburgh, Edinburgh University Press, 2011. ISBN 9781408266663.

Tulloch, John, and Manuel Alvarado, *Doctor Who: The Unfolding Text*. Basingstoke, Macmillan, 1983. ISBN 9780333348482.

Turse, Nick, *Kill Anything That Moves: the Real American War in Vietnam*. New York: Henry Holt, 2013. ISBN 9780805086911.

Walpole, Horace, *The Castle of Otranto*. 1764 .WS Lewis, ed,, Oxford, Oxford University Press, 1998. ISBN 9780192834409.

Periodicals

Daily Mail

Cameron, Haydon, and Hewett, Anthony, 'The Beauty and the

Bovver Girl... Enter Miss World... In a Puff of Smoke'. 21 November 1970.

Lingwood, Louise, 'We'll Smile'. 3 April 1973.

Pigache, Philippa, 'Good news: That's the Verdict on Those BBC Ladies'. 7 September 1972.

Summers, Owen, 'Carr Bombs: Girls Quizzed'. 12 February 1971.

Wilkins, Sally, 'Women's Causes Bore Me Says Barbara Castle'. 9 December 1970.

Daily Mirror

'30,000 Vietnam Men on Heroin'. 30 April 1971.

'Vietnam Revolt'. 13 April 1972.

'Vietnam: Why the silence?' 28 December 1972.

Doctor Who Magazine (DWM) (aka *Doctor Who Monthly*)

'Matrix Data Bank'' DWM #70. November 1982.

Ainsworth, John, 'Elisabeth'. DWM *Special Edition* #23: *Sarah Jane Smith*, October 2009.

Bentham, Jeremy, 'Living in the Past'. DWM #56, September 1981.

Bentham, Jeremy, 'Star Profile: Elisabeth Sladen'. DWM #49, February 1981.

Bentham, Jeremy, 'The Visitation'. DWM #62, March 1982.

Hearn, Marcus, 'The Doctor's Best Friend'. DWM #440, 16 November 2011.

Marson, Richard, 'Elisabeth Sladen'. DWM #89, June 1984.

Marson, Richard and Patrick Mulkern, 'The Pertwee Years'. DWM Winter Special, 1985.

Rigby, Jonathan, 'A Natural Charmer'. DWM #526. July 2018.

The Guardian

Banks-Smith, Nancy and Michael Billington, 'Pygmalion/Second House on Television', 17 December 1973

Daley, Janet [no title]. 1 January 1968.

Duodu, Cameron, 'Land of Black Baddies'. 7 December 1968.

Stott, Mary [no title]. 14 January 1971.

The Observer

Holland, Mary, 'Women's Lib in Focus'. 24 January 1971.

Whitehorn, Katharine, 'Women's Lib: Could It Happen Here?' 14 February 1971.

The Stage

Bilbow, Marjorie, 'Who Else Is There to Blame But the Director?' *The Stage and Television Today*, 6 May 1965.

Henderson, Audrey, 'Basingstoke: The Lion in Winter'. *The Stage and Television Today*, 2 January 1981.

Marriott, RB, 'At Blandings: Wayne, Mount, Hare, Hayter, Pertwee, Lauchlan'. *The Stage and Television Today*, 5 September 1968.

Purser, Ann, 'Success of BBC2's Thriller Serials'. *The Stage and Television Today*, 1 June 1967.

The Times

'Today's Engagements'. *The Times*, 29 May 1971.

'Today's Engagements'. *The Times*. 26 June 1971.

Brittain, Victoria, 'A Conspiracy to Belittle Women's Liberation'. *The Times*. 12 January 1971.

Radcliffe, Michael. 'Fuseli: The Dramatic Moment'. *The Times*, 18 January 1973.

Winton, Malcolm, 'Women's Lib: Maoists, Trotskyites and Mothers in Action'. *The Times*, 19 October 1970.

TARDIS

Langford, Howard D, 'Moral Symbolism in Doctor Who'.*TARDIS* vol 5 #3&4, 1980.

Wiggins, Martin J, 'Artificial History'. *TARDIS* vol 6 # 3&4, October 1981.

Ashton, Nigel J, 'Harold Macmillan and the "Golden Days" of Anglo-American Relations Revisited, 1957–63'. *Diplomatic History*, volume 29 #4, September 2005.

Bates, Margaret L, 'Tanganyika: The Development of a Trust Territory'. *International Organization* volume 9 #1, February 1955.

Bentham, Jeremy, 'Production Office'. *An Adventure in Space and Time #70: The Time Warrior*, 1985.

Bignell, Richard, 'The Original Sarah-Jane Smith'. *Nothing at the End of the Lane* #3, January 2012.

Broders, Simone, 'The Fast and the Curious: The Role of Curiosity in the Gothic Heroine's "Grand Tour of the Mind"'. *English Studies* volume 98 #8, 2017.

Chapman, James, 'The Adventures of Robin Hood and the Origins of the Television Swashbuckler'. *Media History* volume 17 #3, 2011.

Clarke, Arthur C, 'Clarke's Third Law on UFOs'. *Science*, new series, volume 159 #3812, 19 January 1968.

Doctor Who: The Complete History.

> Volume 19: *The Three Doctors, Carnival of Monsters* and *Frontier in Space*, 19 April 2017.

> Volume 20: *Planet of the Daleks, The Green Death* and *The Time Warrior*, 6 April 2016.

> Volume 22: *Robot, The Ark in Space* and *The Sontaran Experiment*, 18 November 2015.

Doctor Who: Radio Times Special, 1973. Reprinted 2003.

'Government Cannot Stop "Brain Drain"'. *The Daily Telegraph*, 12 February 1964.

Hasty, Will, 'Revolutions and Final Solutions: On Enlightenment and its Dialectic in Mark Twain's *A Connecticut Yankee in King Arthur's Court*'. *Arthuriana* volume 24 #2, 2014.

Hutchings, Peter, '"I'm the Girl He Wants to Kill": The "Women in Peril" Thriller in 1970s British Film and Television'. *Visual Culture in Britain* volume 10 #1, 2009.

Nicholson, Helen, 'Women on the Third Crusade'. *Journal of Medieval History* volume 23 #4, 1997.

Osborne, John, 'Death to Gooks'. *The New Republic*. 13 December

1969.

Otto, Ton, 'The Asaro Mudmen: Local Property, Public Culture?' *The Contemporary Pacific* volume 8 #2. 1996.

Parliamentary Debates (Hansard), House of Commons. 13 February 1967.

Petts, Kenneth John, cover illustration. *John Bull*, 9 November 1957.

Pixley, Andrew, 'Frankenstein Vs the Daleks', *The Essential Doctor Who* #12: *Time Travel*, November 2017.

Sheehan, Neil, 'Should We Have War Crime Trials?'. *The New York Times*, 28 March 1971.

Stirling, Helen, 'Girl Talk'. *In-Vision* #17: *Sarah Special*, June 1989.

Wiggins, Martin, 'Out of Time'. *Circus* #9, Spring 2002.

Television

The Adventures of Robin Hood. ITV, 1955-1959.

> *The Coming of Robin Hood*. ATV London, 25 September 1955.

> *The Genius*. ATV London, 13 April 1958.

> *The May Queen*. ATV London, 22 April 1956.

The Adventures of Sir Lancelot. ITV, 1956-1957.

The Adventures of Sir Prancelot. BBC, 1972.

Arthur of the Britons. ITV, 1972-1973.

Blue Peter. BBC, 1958-.

Doctor Who. BBC, 1963-.

The Time Warrior, 1973-74. DVD release, 2007.

'Beginning the End', dir Brendan Sheppard.

Commentary with Elisabeth Sladen, Barry Letts and Terrance Dicks.

The Hand of Fear, 1976. DVD release, 2006.

Commentary with Tom Baker, Elisabeth Sladen, Judith Paris, Bob Baker and Philip Hinchcliffe.

Ivanhoe. BBC, 1970.

Film

Curtiz, Michael, dir, *The Adventures of Robin Hood*. Warner Bros., 1938.

Fisher, Terence, dir, *The Curse of Frankenstein*, Hammer, 1957.

Garnett, Tay, dir, *A Connecticut Yankee in King Arthur's Court*. Paramount, 1949.

Harvey, Anthony, dir, *The Lion in Winter*. Avco Embassy, 1968.

Visual Art

Blake, William, 'The Ghost of a Flea'. 1820.

Fuseli, Henry, 'The Nightmare'. 1781.

Fuseli, Henry, attrib, 'Wrestlers'. 18th or early 19th century.

West, Benjamin, 'The Death of Wolfe'. 1770.

Web

BBC Genome. http://genome.ch.bbc.co.uk/.

High Adventure: The Adventures of Robin Hood, 20 December 1969.
http://genome.ch.bbc.co.uk/b693aae9fa2e4519aa279de01d 82773b. Accessed 30 March 2018.

Holiday 73, 28 December 1972.
http://genome.ch.bbc.co.uk/8a1062b34a384170a9648a163 85f832f. Accessed 31 March 2018.

The Movie Crazy Years: The Adventures of Robin Hood, 9 July 1971.
http://genome.ch.bbc.co.uk/112f6f4c6939497f8825ae0b19 7f88c8. Accessed 30 March 2018.

Pebble Mill at One, 14 January 1974.
https://genome.ch.bbc.co.uk/038f796a831144f4b0d9309a6 361b6e3. Accessed 21 May 2018.

Saturday Cinema: A Connecticut Yankee in King Arthur's Court, 29 December 1973.
https://genome.ch.bbc.co.uk/cbb371a903974f38a2f71d882 8be7c3e. Accessed 14 May 2018.

Tomorrow's World, 24 December 1971.
http://genome.ch.bbc.co.uk/5b3fcc9225d44978985fb634a9 676fa1. Accessed 31 March 2018.

Oxford Dictionary of National Biography.
http://www.oxforddnb.com/.

'Chapman, Frederick Spencer (1907–1971), Explorer and Mountaineer'. https://doi.org/10.1093/ref:odnb/30919. Accessed 6 March 2018.

Kilburn, Matthew, 'Cobham's Cubs (act 1734–1747)'. https://doi.org/10.1093/ref:odnb/93706. Accessed 25 March 2018.

Morris, A. J. A. 'Bottomley, Horatio William (1860–1933), Journalist and Swindler'. https://doi.org/10.1093/ref:odnb/31981. Accessed 12 March 2018.

Power, DJ, 'Bréauté, Sir Falkes de (d 1226), Soldier and Royal Favourite'. https://doi.org/10.1093/ref:odnb/3305. Accessed 25 August 2018.

Raychaudhuri, T, 'Dutt, Romesh Chunder [Rameshchandra Datta] (1848–1909), Administrator in India and Author'. https://doi.org/10.1093/ref:odnb/32943. Accessed 13 July 2018.

Taylor, Miles, 'Bull, John (fl1712-), Fictitious Epitomist of Englishness and British Imperialism'. https://doi.org/10.1093/ref:odnb/68195. Accessed 25 August 2018.

Watson, Fiona, 'Buchan [née Macduff], Isabel, Countess of Buchan (b c1270, d after 1313), Noblewoman'. https://doi.org/10.1093/ref:odnb/54144. Accessed 23 May 2018.

Watson, Fiona, 'Dunbar, Patrick, Eighth Earl of Dunbar or of March, and Earl of Moray (1285-1369), Soldier and Magnate'. https://doi.org/10.1093/ref:odnb/8206. Accessed 23 May 2018.

Oxford English Dictionary. http://www.oed.com/.

'gook, n.'. January 2018.
http://www.oed.com/view/Entry/80017/. Accessed 20
March 2018.

'osmic', Oxford English Dictionary search page,
http://www.oed.com/search?searchType=dictionary&q=osm
ic. Accessed 18 July 2018.

'murder, v.' (sense 9). March 2018.
http://www.oed.com/view/Entry/123859/. Accessed 19 May
2018.

'tail, n.1.', senses 5a, 5c, 5d. March 2018.
http://www.oed.com/view/Entry/197067/. Accessed 25 May
2018.

'taille, n.', sense 1. March 2018.
www.oed.com/view/Entry/197087/. Accessed 25 May 2018.

'jingo, int., and n., and adj.'. June 2018.
www.oed.com/view/Entry/101343/. Accessed 26 August
2018

'Armour: Domaru (1570)'. Royal Armouries.
https://collections.royalarmouries.org/object/rac-object-
30423.html. Accessed 19 August 2018.

'Obituaries: Harvey Unna'. *The Times*, 5 August 2003.
https://www.thetimes.co.uk/article/harvey-unna-9kv36wfppk7
Accessed 10 May 2018.

Ashfield, Steve, '**Doctor Who**: The Curse of Peladon'. *Television Heaven*, May 2014.
http://www.televisionheaven.co.uk/curse_of_peladon.htm.

Accessed 24 March 2018.

Bahn, Christopher, '**Doctor Who** (Classic): *The Curse of Peladon*'. AV/TV Club, 1 April 2012. https://tv.avclub.com/doctor-who-classic-the-curse-of-peladon-1798172220. Accessed 24 March 2018.

Bainbridge, Timothy, 'Romantic artists'. *The Spectator*, 24 March 1973. http://archive.spectator.co.uk/article/24th-march-1973/16/romantic-artists. Accessed 27 March 2018.

Braxton, Mark, 'Inferno'. **Doctor Who** Story Guide, *Radio Times*. http://www.radiotimes.com/news/2009-10-06/inferno/. Accessed 27 March 2018.

Clark, Finn, 'A Review' http://www.pagefillers.com/dwrg/timew.htm#13. Accessed 6 September 2018.

'Clement Attlee at 80: Archive, 1963', *The Guardian*, 3 January 2017 (3 January 1963). https://www.theguardian.com/politics/2017/jan/03/clement-attlee-labour-leader-1963-archive. Accessed 3 May 2018.

Foster, AJ, and EE Cuthell, *The Robber Baron of Bedford Castle*. 1903. Project Gutenberg. http://www.gutenberg.org/ebooks/44374/ Accessed 24 August 2018.

Elisabeth Sladen on Screen. https://sites.google.com/site/elisabethsladenonscreen/home/. Accessed 19 May 2018.

Ford, Joe, 'The Time Warrior written by Robert Holmes and directed by Alan Bromley (sic)'.

https://docohobigfinish.blogspot.com/2013/08/the-time-warrior-written-by-robert.html. Accessed 6 September 2018

'Freddie Spencer Chapman'. Wikipedia. https://en.wikipedia.org/wiki/Freddie_Spencer_Chapman. Accessed 6 March 2018.

Fuseli, Henry, attrib, 'Wrestlers'. 18th to early 19th century. British Museum, Artstor. http://ezproxy-prd.bodleian.ox.ac.uk:3051/asset/AGERNSHEIMIG_10313158890. Accessed 13 June 2018.

Hadoke, Toby, 'Marcia Wheeler: Part 1'. **Toby Hadoke's Who's Round** #84. https://www.bigfinish.com/releases/v/toby-hadoke-s-who-s-round-84---marcia-wheeler-part-1-1174. Accessed 3 August 2018.

Hood, Stuart, 'Who Does It?' *The Spectator,* 14 March 1969. http://archive.spectator.co.uk/article/14th-march-1969/11/who-does-it. Accessed 19 March 2018.

Hunt, W, 'John (1167?-1216). king of England'. *Dictionary of National Biography*, 1885-1900, Volume 29. https://en.wikisource.org/wiki/John_(1167%3F-1216)_(DNB00). Accessed 26 August 2018.

Martin, Dan, 'Elisabeth Sladen dies at 65'. *The Guardian*, 20 April 2011. https://www.theguardian.com/tv-and-radio/2011/apr/19/elisabeth-sladen-doctor-who-star-dies. Accessed 18 May 2018.

Pentland, Gordon, 'The Eglinton Tournament 1839: A Victorian take on the Anglo-Scottish rivalry'. *History of Parliament*, 4 September 2014.

https://thehistoryofparliament.wordpress.com/2014/09/04/the-eglinton-tournament-1839-a-victorian-take-on-the-anglo-scottish-rivalry/. Accessed 31 March 2018.

Photograph of Patricia Driscoll. https://commons.wikimedia.org/wiki/File:Patricia_Driscoll_-_The_Adventures_of_Robin_Hood,_Vol._1,_No._8.jpg. Accessed 20 May 2018.

Pick, Hella, 'Lord Weidenfeld Obituary'. *The Guardian*, 20 January 2016. https://www.theguardian.com/books/2016/jan/20/lord-weidenfeld. Accessed 10 May 2018.

Reuben, Susan, 'Paddington Bear: His Secret Jewish Heritage'. The JC. 29 June 2017, https://www.thejc.com/comment/comment/paddington-bear-his-secret-jewish-heritage-1.440729. Accessed 10 May 2018.

Thompson, Kathryn, 'Godebog!'. *The Redress of the Past: Historical Pageants in Britain*, 18 April 2016. http://www.historicalpageants.ac.uk/publications/blog/godebog-kathryn-thompson/. Accessed 20 April 2018.

Twain, Mark, *A Connecticut Yankee in King Arthur's Court*. 1889. Project Gutenberg .http://www.gutenberg.org/ebooks/86. Accessed 26 August 2018.

Wicks, Kevin, 'Elisabeth Sladen, Sarah Jane from **Doctor Who**, has died at 63'. *Anglophenia,* April 2011. http://www.bbcamerica.com/anglophenia/2011/04/elisabeth-sladen-sarah-jane-from-doctor-who-has-died-at-63/. Accessed 18 May 2018.

Yates, Ronald E, 'WW II Die-hards Receive Cool Greeting In Japan'.

Chicago Tribune, 15 January 1990.
http://articles.chicagotribune.com/1990-01-
15/news/9001040661_1_japanese-soldiers-and-civilians-japanese-
people-wartime. Accessed 11 March 2018.

BIOGRAPHY

Matthew Kilburn has been writing about **Doctor Who** in one way or another for well over 40 years, probably since he first put crayon to paper. In recent years he has written for *Doctor Who: 50 Years*, *The Essential Doctor Who* and *Doctor Who Magazine Special Edition* and contributed production notes for two BBC DVD **Doctor Who** releases, *Planet of Giants* and the special edition of *The Aztecs*. He has also contributed to books such as *Time And Relative Dissertations In Space*, *Inside Out* and *The Eleventh Hour*. He has written for several fanzines over the decades including *Skaro*, *Circus*, *Faze*, *This Way Up*, *Panic Moon*, *The Terrible Zodin* and *Vworp Vworp!* as well as contributed reviews to *The Doctor Who News Page*. He has for two periods in its history been editor of the Oxford University-based **Doctor Who** fanzine, *The Tides of Time*. He's written on other television series too, including **Star Trek: The Next Generation** and **The Paper Lads**.

Away from **Doctor Who**, if there really is such a thing, Matthew has a doctorate in 18th-century British history, has worked for several major humanities research projects, having been a research editor for several years at the *Oxford Dictionary of National Biography*, a research officer at *The History of Parliament: The Lords 1660-1715*, and a freelance contributor and researcher for both projects and for the *Oxford English Dictionary*. He contributed three chapters to *The History of Oxford University Press: Volume I*, edited by Ian Gadd, and is currently working on a book chapter on the parliamentary representation and local government of Chippenham. He is originally from north-east England, but lives in Oxfordshire.